The Opening Door

The Opening Door

Our Experience of God

NIGEL COLLINSON

'It is not the experiences which are important,
but the one who has been experienced in them.'
                                    Jürgen Moltmann

EPWORTH PRESS

© Nigel Collinson 1986

All rights reserved. No part of this publication may be reproduced, stored in a retrieval system, or transmitted, in any form or by any means, electronic, mechanical, photocopying, recording or otherwise, without the prior permission of the publisher, Epworth Press.

British Library Cataloguing in Publication Data
Collinson, Nigel
  The opening door: our experience of God.
  1. God
  I. Title
  231   BT102

ISBN 0–7162–0416–9

First published 1986
by Epworth Press
Room 190, 1 Central Buildings
Westminster, London SW1H 9NR

Typeset by Gloucester Typesetting Services
and printed in Great Britain by
Richard Clay (The Chaucer Press) Ltd
Bungay, Suffolk

To Lorna

Contents

Preface — ix

1   The Silence of God — 1
    (a) Where is God? — 4
    (b) Our buried life — 8
    (c) Waiting in patience — 15
   Conclusion — 21

2   The Ambiguity of God — 23
    (a) A case of mistaken identity — 24
    (b) Power — 28
    (c) Ministry — 34
   Conclusion — 41

3   The Presence of God — 43
    (a) God in relationships — 45
    (b) God the story — 53
    (c) God at the limits — 62
   Conclusion — 69

4   Our Response to God — 71
    (a) Prodigal sons and daughters — 72
    (b) Commonplace spirituality — 77
    (c) Faith — 83
   Conclusion — 90

Notes — 93

Preface

Two incidents compelled me to set about writing this book. Driving through the Cotswolds from Oxford to Worcester on an absolutely perfect October day, a question slipped into my mind. 'How do I speak about God on such a day as this? Where is he?' Week by week, I encourage people to thank God, to pray to him for their needs and the needs of others, but when it comes down to it, what does it really mean to talk about God's presence in the world and how do we experience him?

Normally, I would have headed off the question, assured myself that I knew the answer already, but did not have the time to explain it to myself fully at that particular moment. This question would not go away however. 'Come on,' it insisted, 'address yourself to me. If you can't answer me, you have no right to go on speaking about God the way you do.'

The second incident was one of those family conversations you sometimes have at Christmas or on a slack summer evening. This was Christmas and our thoughts turned to religion and the obvious gap between what people actually believe and what traditional Christianity expects them to believe.

Preface

'God's just an idea to get you through life!' someone remarked. The words stung. Is that what I had spent half my adult life trying to serve – just an idea? Eventually I came to ask myself what was wrong with an idea, especially if it was a good one. After all, ideas make the world go round. But there was a case to be answered. Is God just the figment of religious imagination?

My growing conviction has been that what happens to people will tell us as much as we can know about God, idea or not. As the Jewish theologian, Martin Buber, put it, 'What happens does not happen in a vacuum existing between God and the individual. The Word travels by way of the individual to the people.'[1]

The best evidence for God is found in the stories people tell about him out of their own experience, although those stories may not necessarily be obviously 'religious'. You find them in many places, newspapers, television, books, pieces of autobiography, snatches of conversation and so on. The Word has indeed become flesh.

There is a picture in the Louvre by the seventeenth-century painter Georges de la Tour called *St Joseph the Carpenter*. In a halo of darkness, lit only by a candle, Joseph is bending over a piece of wood, hard at work. At his side is the boy who holds the candle, shielding the flame from the draught with his hand. You can almost hear Joseph calling out, 'Bring the candle closer, lad, I need more light!'

We do well to recall that at the heart of the Christian faith there was a divine sharing in commonplace and homely things; a candle in a boy's hand, shielded from the wind, which has continued to illuminate our path to God.

I am indebted to many people who have contributed to this

Preface

book, either directly or indirectly. In addition to those acknowledged in the Notes, there are conversations, letters and words of encouragement, all of which have been of great assistance. Not the least important has been the helpfulness of the staff of the Theology Faculty Library at Pusey House, Oxford.

Finally, I would like to thank Dorothy Stepney for her patience and kindness in typing the manuscript.

Biblical quotations, except where noted in the text, are from *The New English Bible*, Second Edition 1970, used by permission of Oxford and Cambridge University Presses.

1 *The Silence of God*

It may sound an odd thing to say in this latter part of the twentieth century, but I believe that many people have an experience of God. We do not always appreciate it or make the most of it. Sometimes this experience of God will come like a bolt from the blue, which cannot be ignored. More often, it will come quietly and unobtrusively, as quietly and as unobtrusively as when you sit reading or talking with friends and the door silently opens.

I say that many men and women have this experience of God because I profoundly believe that in parallel with the tangible world which is all around us and plain to see, there is, as it were, another world – the realm of spiritual things, of eternity, of God. At times, the dividing wall between these two worlds becomes transparent. A door opens, and a man or woman with feet very firmly on the ground may catch a glimpse of God.

Many people have experienced this opening of doors. It is said that the early Christian martyrs received the Beatific Vision at the moment of their death. Certainly many sensitive men and women, the poets, the writers, the musicians and the

The Opening Door

painters, as they probed the depths of human experience, have discovered even greater depths. Doors have opened for them to express in words, in music, in texture and in colour more truth than we are capable of understanding in the cold light of day. Handel spoke for them all as he wrote his *Messiah*: 'I saw all heaven before my eyes.' Kepler the astronomer exclaimed, 'I was thinking God's thoughts after him.' On the last sheet of the original score of his *Dream of Gerontius* Edward Elgar wrote these words of John Ruskin:

> This is the best of me: for the rest, I ate and drank and slept and loved and hated like another:
> but this I *saw* and *know*
> this if anything of mine is worth your memory.[1]

Belief in God has become increasingly problematical in our century and yet, curiously, the idea of God will not go away. He survives the atheist rigours of the Communist east as he proves more than a match for the debilitating affluence of the capitalist west. Now, for increasing numbers of people, he comes at us, against all our expectations, from the direction of the world's forgotten poor. Try as we may, we cannot lose him.

Nevertheless, there are questions remaining. For the God who makes himself known is not the highly formalized unchanging God of the Creeds, nor is he wholly to be contained within the descriptions and activities of one religion. And, despite my figurative use of parallel worlds, God does not come at us from 'outside', from his world to ours. That implies that the two are separate and that the former is almost certainly more important than the latter. There is only one world available to us but as we perceive its deeper meaning so doors open and we recognize the God who is the depth

The Silence of God

beyond depth. In just the same way, a painting may be a collection of pigments and shapes or it may be a great work, an articulate statement of something which is always true.

Inevitably, what we know of God will be partial and distorted by the very experiences that bring him to us, or us to him. That is why some of the greatest masters of the search have counselled humility before the great Silence. 'God is above both space and time and name and conception,' said Clement of Alexandria.

We want to know and yet there is a refraction, we suspect, that takes place between the reality of the great Silence and our experiencing it. The presence of God in commonplace, ordinary things is like sunlight shining through a piece of glass. Even as it does so, the light is refracted, angled out of true by the very thing that brought it to our attention in the first place. Shelley expressed this same truth when he wrote:

> The One remains, the many change and pass;
> Heaven's light forever shines, Earth's shadows fly;
> Life, like a dome of many-coloured glass,
> Stains the white radiance of Eternity.[2]

The more one presses the question 'How do we experience God?', the more one is driven to try to understand, no matter how feebly, who it is that confronts us. We commonly speak of this person behaving 'in character' or that person behaving 'out of character'. We may not rule out the possibility of surprise but we generally recognize that people will be true to their nature in their dealings with us. So we are led to ask, 'What sort of God confronts us like this? What sort of landscape does the gently opening door reveal?'

The Opening Door

(a) Where is God?

It is a question commonly asked by those who believe in him. If you have looked into the eyes of the cancer patient, held the hand of the woman whose husband has just been tragically killed, stood beside bewildered parents unable to understand why their child has gone wrong, or acted as go-between for the couple whose marriage is breaking up all around them, you have heard the question asked: 'Where is God?' Sometimes it remains unspoken, hanging in the air like some motionless balloon with no sudden breeze to hurry it away. 'Where is God in all this?'

Alert student minds will soon ask the question, particularly those trained in the natural sciences. It is not that they believe science answers all questions. They have botched too many experiments, they know the sheer cussedness of the material they are working with to expect the results always to come out right. Yet they have been trained to see the world, things as they are, as a linked series of physical events which can, in principle, be described and understood. Small wonder now the cosmologists are probing the first milliseconds of the Big Bang that some ask whether or not there is room for God.

People question the idea of God out of their own experience. Many are happy to put things down to 'the will of God' or to talk about him as if he were actually 'there', like a piece of furniture. But there are those for whom God is, at best, an idea which gets you through life, a very important idea because getting through is important, but an idea nonetheless. There is nothing in reality which corresponds to the idea.

People such as these do not see themselves as spiritually deprived in any way. On the contrary, they are often sensitive, morally-aware, life-affirming men and women who make

The Silence of God

an extraordinarily valuable contribution to their community – and often to their church! However, they find God, as he is talked about in the church, unnecessary, incomprehensible, trivial or impossibly remote. They have done their own thinking, measuring the world-view which they and their contemporaries hold, with its vastly stretched horizons, against the world-view which the old theology appears to offer them and the latter seems oddly out of touch with what they know by experience. On their lips the question 'Where is God?' has already been answered in the negative.

The problem of God is partly a problem of words. Words to describe someone we have been taught to think of as beyond description are bound to be hard to find. In any case, the words we use in everyday speech have their origin in everyday things rather than in the mysteries of God. But even in everyday speech words are not always easy to find. They say too much or not enough. Words have a peculiar knack of changing meaning between speaker and hearer. They are facts and poems all in the same breath. They draft legal documents and, if you wish them to, will write letters of sympathy or love. Words have spaces round them. Into those spaces we pour meaning. The poet is especially good at exploiting the spaces. By using familiar words in unfamiliar ways he conjures new meaning. Equally good with words are politicians, barristers, reporters and interviewers. Words are their stock-in-trade. They know when their words need to be precise, have edge, be incisive. They know too when to leave just enough space around their words to put the question or hint at a deeper meaning.

Unfortunately, it is difficult to have such a sure touch with our words about God. The literalist wants to be too precise and sure, an approach which many find unappealing. It is

The Opening Door

equally possible to go to the other extreme and use words so loosely, give them so much space, that they have no meaning at all.

Despite all our difficulties with words about him, however, the real problem lies with God himself, because so often he appears to remain resolutely in the background. He is not obvious. Often he actually seems to provoke the question, 'Where is he?'

In January 1983, Charles Elliott, former Director of Christian Aid, broadcast a series of talks following a visit that he had made to Central America. He described a conversation with a group of refugees who had been caught up in the fighting in El Salvador:

> They talked of their faith and of how they tried to encourage each other to hang on to that faith in a loving God whose kingdom was coming, in spite of all the evidence to the contrary. They described the experiences they had been through. Some had seen their families killed before their eyes. Some had seen their children die as they fled through the mountains. Some had seen whole villages bombed out of existence. One man in the group broke down and shuffled away. I found him afterwards and we talked some more. His experience had not been very different from that of the others. He had lost both wife and child and was desperate to go and see if he could find them, but he knew that if he did, it was unlikely he would get a mile from the camp before being picked up. I asked him if he found any comfort or help in the faith of the rest of the refugees. He didn't say anything for a bit and then he simply said 'God is silent.'[3]

'God is silent.' What more eloquent cry of despair could you find than that, faced with the God who so resolutely remains in the background? I have heard it expressed differently. He is absent, some say. He still has his being in eternity but he has withdrawn himself from this world. Others, particularly the philosophers, say God is idle. By that they do not mean that he is feckless, unwilling to work, but that despite the Christian affirmations of his power and his love, neither seems to match up to reality, so we might as well do without him. It is the theological equivalent of crying 'Wolf'. We say many things about God but when we look for him he is not obviously there.

The mystery is an old one. The writers of the Old Testament felt it just as much as we do. The unknown Psalmist demanded: 'Rest not, O God; O God, be neither silent nor still' (Psalm 83). The middle chapter of the prophet Isaiah, that great flowering of religious insight, strikes a familiar chord:

> Surely God is among you and there is no other,
> no other God.
> How then canst thou be a god that hidest thyself,
> O God of Israel, the deliverer? (Isa. 45.15)

We should not imagine that the hiddenness of God is a minor intrusion into the Old Testament, the cry of a discontented few in hard times. In a recent book Robert Davidson has shown that it is an important and recurring theme.[4]

'Where is God?' The way we answer that question has as much to do with our expectations as with God himself. Always there will be the tussle between being sure and not sure. No matter how much we long to be certain, to look for clear evidence of his activity, our experience of God will mostly be fleeting, elusive, ambiguous, because that appears to be his nature.

The Opening Door

Light-years away from the El Salvador refugee, in circumstances if not in belief, someone recently wrote of her experience of God in a personal letter:

> It seems to me that God is that fine area of ground, so glorious you know it to be, that you catch very fleetingly as you come from the sunshine into rather a lot of cloud before you land at Heathrow. You have the window-seat, you eagerly wait to get through the clouds; and just once or twice you do see a bit of land; 'Was that . . . yes, it was . . . was that the London Docks, was that Kew Bridge . . . oh I wish the dratted clouds would go away; I'll never know for sure now.' And you peer and strain but never can you repeat that glimpse.
>
> God is like this for me . . . every so often there is the most exciting glimpse, a flash frame. And yes, you have a broader feeling that the ground is there beneath the cloud, you just know it's there.

Such an experience will be of little use to those who demand certainty, who have a fixed idea of a God who is always in control. There are those, however, who have heard the Silence of God, and catch in it the echoes of a baby's cry before the dawn, a baby born to a carpenter's wife, and who discern there, too, the hiddenness of God, the opening of doors.

(b) Our buried life

In the New Town there is a rather beautiful eighteenth-century parish church. Set in the town square, it is surrounded by fine houses of a similar period, houses that once would have been occupied by the leading townsfolk of the day. Until comparatively recently, that square would have been

The Silence of God

the hub of the wheel, the community would have revolved around it and the church which dominates the square would have 'stood for something'. Its very presence, let alone its worship and its way of life, was a symbol of the larger map on which the townsfolk lived, a map in which God figured prominently. The people may not have been avid churchgoers; neither would they have been any better or more 'Christian' than we are. But at least within their firmament God had an unshakeable place. They thanked him quite naturally at harvest time and on the occasion of a victory or a new birth. They prayed to him in times of extremity, perhaps more in hope than expectation but, nonetheless, he was there and he would at least listen.

When the New Town planners got to work they decided to locate the town centre elsewhere, less than a mile away in fact, but decidedly 'elsewhere'. It was 'elsewhere' that the new shopping precinct was built; all the new roads led to 'elsewhere'. The result is that 'elsewhere' is where everybody now is and our eighteenth-century square with its church stands quiet, on the fringe, isolated and unnecessary.

There are those who would see this as an epitaph for God or, if not quite as final as that, a parable of his decline. Indeed, that is sometimes how it has seemed from inside the church, the culmination of a process of doubt which began more than a century ago with the new approach to science and the Bible. Charles Darwin's autobiography is a sad record of the price he paid for his scientific achievement. First, he tells us, he lost his love of music, then his sense of wonder and finally his consciousness of God.

More up-to-date evidence comes from Michael Goulder, until recently an Anglican priest and theologian, who has described his own loss of faith in a moving essay entitled 'The

The Opening Door

Fram Abandoned'. The Fram was the boat in which the Norwegian explorer, Nansen, tried to reach the North Pole, an attempt which he had to abandon, leaving the Fram to the rigours of the ice.

Michael Goulder had started out with what he calls 'a redblooded theology', a belief in a God who was actually there if only you looked in the right place, a God who answered prayer unmistakably, who acted to put things right or alter the course of events for the better. Gradually, he felt the difficulties of such a faith in the light of experience. Each experience caused him to question or to modify his 'redblooded theology' until in the end there was nothing left. He writes:

> So sick at heart, I turned my huskies southwards. My Pole had been a will-o-the-wisp. My Fram, my beloved church, was locked for ever in the ice-floes of theological contradiction, a barren and chilling waste. My thirty years of high endeavour had been an error. Nevertheless, I think no endeavour that engages the best one has to give is wasted. I do not repent of my quest. I have brought home much rich experience from my journey and helped others on my way. I wrote to the Bishop of Birmingham on St Matthew's Day 1981, to resign my orders; and in fact to leave the church.[5]

Michael Goulder is speaking for many who have been nurtured on the idea that God is in some way actually identifiable as a separate being, a force to be reckoned with, one who does things unmistakably. His poignant statement affirms that what we know by experience does not match up to what traditional Christian theology has been telling us. However, behind Michael Goulder's metaphor of the great explorer's

The Silence of God

boat left behind to the ravages of the ice and the weather, one senses a real regret at high purpose abandoned.

Matthew Arnold, Darwin's contemporary, for all his impatience with dogma and creed, retained his faith in God. His poems are full of regret and sadness at the difficulties which beset religious faith and the sheer loss of abandoning it. In one he wrote:

> But often, in the world's most crowded streets,
> But often, in the din of strife,
> There rises an unspeakable desire
> After the knowledge of our buried life.[6]

Why does Matthew Arnold speak of a life which is buried? What does the phrase 'our buried life' imply?

First of all, it is a part of us. There is nothing nearer to us than life. We might describe life differently, it may have a different content as between one person and another, but 'my life' is as near to saying 'me' as I can possibly get. Matthew Arnold speaks of this 'life' as a corporate possession; it is ours. He is indicating then, something which is part of us as human beings; it is at once deeply personal but held in common with others. And, because there is the note of sadness in his words, it is something which once, at least, was felt to be important.

But it has become buried.

Things become buried for all sorts of reasons. An old tractor on a farm is put behind the barn because the farmer has bought a new and better one. Gradually, the old one is forgotten, becomes rusty and unserviceable, surrounded by nettles and bindweed. It may stay there for ever and rot or it may be discovered by the enthusiast, taken away and restored. Its loss, as its discovery, was almost casual. The ring lost on the beach and buried in the sand, the crock of Roman coins, the

The Opening Door

Viking helmet turned up in the field or found in a stream, were all buried accidentally and awaited the sharp-eyed passer-by or the earnest men with their metal detectors. Their loss and their discovery alike are accidental.

The incriminating evidence buried in the garden, a community's treasures hidden in the face of a besieging army, the riches of a dead Pharaoh, these were buried deliberately, in haste or in secret or with great public solemnity.

And what of the great and ancient city, whose only evidence now is a few humps and ditches and scattered stones, or a rocky mound jutting out of the desert landscape which seems to have been there from the beginning but of which the archeologist tells a different tale? Was its loss casual, or accidental or deliberate? How many years does it take to bury a city?

So too that thing of importance, 'our life' as the poet describes it, has become buried, deliberately, accidentally, casually. It has become overlaid by other concerns which seemed more pressing, more important at the time. Its overlaying perhaps took years, so that we did not realize what was happening, or it was lost in an instant, overnight, jettisoned as one would a cargo that had shifted in a heavy sea.

And yet, not quite, because like most buried things it is still capable of being found. It is not something which decays, rots, tumbles down. It can be buried, hidden, lost, abandoned or ignored but it has the capacity to persist and, against all the odds, to make its presence felt, whether 'in the world's most crowded streets' or in the moment of solitariness.

It is this 'buried life' which, I believe, corresponds to the hiddenness of God. What we experience as buried, half-felt, inarticulate, or at the mercy of the wit or cynic, is the counterpart, or more accurately the rippling seismic shock, of the one who is happy to hide himself in man, not as a

The Silence of God

temporary disguise, but as a last resort, a permanent disclosure.

The journalist Bel Mooney has described her own desire for God in an article headed, significantly enough, 'Scapegoat in a Country Churchyard'.[7] She had rejected the idea of God early on. In a world so devoid of love, how could she believe in a God of love? Yet the longing for God persisted and in many ways the longing has become more important than the possessing. She writes: 'Now it seems more interesting to consider the longing itself, and establish its truth. It is a slow and patient exploration in which the loneliness and doubts of the journey are far more important than any ecstatic arrival at Ithaca.'

Where does the journey take her? It goes by way of Augustine of Hippo's struggles and T. S. Eliot's 'last desert'. It leads via the country churchyard and the church porch 'with its Brownie poster and flower rota, and essential churchyard rules'. It embraces George Eliot's 'religion of humanity' in which she combined both reason and reverence, believing 'that our moral progress may be measured by the degree in which we sympathise with individual suffering and individual joy'.

Bel Mooney too has her experiences of God, but for her the doors open on to a landscape that is different from how she imagined God to be, different too from what religion taught her to expect.

> When I read Wordsworth's defiance in the Prelude:
>
>> 'Dust as we are, the immortal spirit grows
>> Like harmony in music . . .'
>
> or listen to Haydn's *Seven Last Words*, or the *St Matthew Passion*, I know what it is to experience an epiphany, but

it inevitably expresses itself as this question: If I abandon all effort, and feeling part of the whole, rejoice in *your* existence, who is to say that in approaching *you* I am not approaching God?

I suspect that Matthew Arnold would have responded in the affirmative and that in turn Bel Mooney would have understood his wistful longing after 'our buried life'. Moreover, I suspect that she would find many friends both inside and outside the churches who themselves count the journey more important than the so-called arrival, impatient as they are with dogma, and incredulous too. Yet they sense the ultimate mystery, the magnetic pull of 'our buried life'. Bel Mooney uses the word 'numinous' to describe it:

> . . . a mystery that hovers at the perimeter of our comprehension . . . it is that faculty which links more people than one might think, in an age such as this, and which serves to intensify moments of pagan joy. It is that sense, and the conviction that there is more to *us* than getting and spending, that takes me (and my doubt) into the village church, to keep silent during the Creed, yet to admit by my presence the power of old stones, old faith.

One of the oldest story-lines in the world is that of the buried treasure which a person stumbles upon by accident. Jesus himself used it although he was by no means the first. For him it became a symbol of the importance of the Kingdom of Heaven, for which a person would sell everything. But usually treasure has to be dug for and in the digging we are not sure how much we shall find or even whether someone has been there before us.

There is uncertainty to the last in digging for buried treasure, just as there will be in the fleeting experiences of God which I have called the unobtrusive opening of a door through which we glimpse a greater truth.

(c) Waiting in patience

Patience does not have a very good image. It's for fishermen, chess-players and the trainers of animals. The rest of us are unlikely to put it top of the list of those qualities we admire. We like to get things done. We can manage quite well without patience, or at least with a modicum of it. The phrase that springs most readily to mind, the patience of Job, sounds unpromisingly dull, implying, as it does, putting up with things, taking what comes and making the best of it. This is not at all the kind of patience we will need if we are to discover the signs of God's presence.

Simone Weil was a French philosopher who through her friendship with a Roman Catholic priest, Father Perrin, was drawn increasingly to faith out of a background of atheism. Yet she always remained an outsider so far as the Roman Catholic Church was concerned. She was never baptized and so never received the Sacrament. In one of her letters to Father Perrin, dated 19 January 1942, Simone Weil wrote:

> I cannot help still wondering whether in these days when so large a proportion of humanity is sunk in materialism, God does not want there to be some men and women who have given themselves to him and to Christ and who yet remain outside the Church.[8]

In another letter she said:

> I should betray the truth, that is to say the aspect of truth that I see, if I left the point where I have been since my

The Opening Door

birth, at the intersection of Christianity and everything that is not Christianity.

I have always remained at this exact point, on the threshold of the Church without moving, quite still in patience.[9]

It is hard for us to imagine that anyone might have a vocation, for that is what it is, to remain 'outside' the church, on 'the threshold'. Simone Weil was aware, however, that her knowledge and experience of 'everything that is not Christianity' put her in a position where she could interpret faith to unfaith and, just as important, where she could explain to faith what it was like not to believe. It was an uncomfortable position to be in and she pursued her vocation without the help and support either of the fellowship of the church or of the sacraments. That is why 'patience' was so important. She saw herself, literally, waiting patiently for God.

Increasingly I come to understand that Simone Weil was right because patience is one of those human virtues which corresponds to something which is a part of God, indeed, which even finds its origin in him.

God is not often disclosed in a blinding flash of light. Anyone looking for a quick fix, a ready-made religious experience, is almost bound to be disappointed. This does not stop people looking, however, and neither does it stop people offering a God who is immediately available, often in a white-hot emotional atmosphere. The problems almost always arise later when experience does not match expectations. How can they? Did not one of the finest voices of the Old Testament describe God as the one who hides himself?

It is to understand such a God as this that one must wait patiently. Patience, in fact, is not simply a human quality that we bring to the long search, it is something which corresponds

The Silence of God

to a part of God himself. For instance, when I reflect upon what Christians say about the creativity of God, I am struck by the overwhelming maleness of our understanding. God's creative activity is nearly always associated with masculinity. It is sudden, explosive, external. Invariably we think of God creating with an authoritative word, a divine 'Let there be . . .', a powerful energizing of something new and separate. True enough, the most recent thinking about evolution suggests that new things came to be not by the gradual process of modification normally associated with the word 'evolution' but in sudden bursts of activity after prolonged periods of stability, a random mutation finding an entirely new direction after a time of relative standstill. The masculine image of God's creativity is not out of place in such a modern understanding of life and its origins.

But to concentrate on the sudden bursts of activity alone is to miss the importance of the prolonged periods of waiting, of those vast aeons when nothing stunningly new and exciting was happening except, and it is not a small thing, that life was constantly coming to birth. And in all this coming to birth, at least amongst a very significant section of living things, creativity is expressed not as something explosive and outwards, but as quiet and inwards. Not everything about feminine creativity can be described as receptive, patient waiting, but at least to describe it so illuminates a profound truth. Creativity, for the most part, is two-sided. It is both male and female in its nature, it is active and it is passive, giving and receiving, urgent initiating and patient waiting. This is not to say that patience is entirely a feminine characteristic and activity a masculine one. It is simply to say that for the female, a part of creativity is expressed inwardly and includes a large measure of waiting patiently.

The Opening Door

We have a long history of aversion to anything but the maleness of God. When a crucifixion statue by the sculptor Edwina Sandys, presenting Jesus Christ as a woman, went on display in the Episcopalian Cathedral of St John the Divine in New York at Easter 1984, the Suffragan Bishop of New York was reported as saying that the statue was 'theologically and historically indefensible'.[10]

The line of defence, however, runs by way of Julian of Norwich, the fourteenth-century woman mystic who spoke of the femininity of God, to the book of Proverbs where in chapter 8 the female person of Wisdom is seen as God's companion, remarkably, in creation.

At least glimpsing the feminine aspects of creativity helps us in two ways. In the first place we are enabled to see that what is created can be within its creator, as the embryo is within its mother. Traditionally, we have talked about the creativity of God as if he, at some far-distant point, flung the universe and everything in it into space as a child will throw a ball into the air. Such a belief, with all its associated ideas about the way God is supposed to continue keeping things in order and intervening to put things right, rings hollow in modern ears.

But suppose that creation is a process of coming to be within the creator, for the most part patiently but with spasmodic bursts of energy which push the whole process in a totally new direction. We are then working with a different picture of creativity, particularly if we can bear with the idea that the material in which the creator is working is not totally within his control. Such seems to be the case for how else can unwarranted disease be explained? We are then close to the idea of God disclosed by Jesus, who is enmeshed in the ordinary grittiness of human life, who is overtaken by defeat and pain,

The Silence of God

but who, in a sudden burst of energy, discovers new direction so that the defeat and pain find fresh and deeper meaning.

Therefore, creation from within, and recreation too, can become very helpful ways of reflecting upon God's relationship to our world once we have got away from the idea that all creation is external, majestic, instant.

In the second place, this different aspect of creativity points us to how best we might understand God. The God who works patiently from within must be received patiently. Someone once said to me, 'Prove that the resurrection happened and I'll become a Christian.' How could I? It was starting at the wrong end, like trying to build a skyscraper with no knowledge of structural engineering. Others will say, 'I've tried to pray but nothing ever happens. It doesn't seem to work for me. It's useless.'

We are impatient with God. We want him all at once or not at all. Our expectations demand that he is either there and obviously so, or that he is simply an idea best discarded.

The experience of God, however, needs to be built with patience and from very small beginnings. The great river was not always great. It began as a spring up in the hills, several hundreds or thousands of miles inland. It almost dried up in the rainless season, but the trickle became a stream and it was fed by other streams until it became a river. In places it was shallow and straight. Elsewhere, its course was deep and winding and all the time it was being added to by tributary rivers until finally it met the sea.

Such is the experience of God. It has its beginning in small things but it is fed by all the different experiences of pain and joy, of frustration and fulfilment. From time to time, and always unexpectedly, a door will quietly open and we will respond to a reality beyond sight and sound. But for the most part we will be without any great confirmations of his presence, simply getting on with the business of building relationships, doing our daily work, giving and receiving. There will be times of exhilaration and times of set-back, times when things make sense and times when life seems wasteful and without purpose. These things are common to us all but to wait patiently upon God means that we give ourselves the opportunity to make connexions, 'to see into the life of things'. This is especially true of those times when faith is hard going, when all seems aridly useless or when doubt threatens to swamp us.

Frederick Borsch in his superb book *Power in Weakness*, in which he discusses some of the miracle stories of the gospels, talks about blind Bartimaeus waiting in his darkness by the road side and compares it to his own moments of darkness when God seems far away.

> I have learned that in the night there is little I can do but huddle and wait. Sometimes the darkness seems endless, so cold that the breath of my wordless prayer is but a vapour. I try to remember the poet's words:
>
> > 'I said to my soul be still, and let the dark come upon you
> > Which shall be the darkness of God'   (East Coker)
>
> And then miraculously, once more the daystar rises and life returns. Perhaps on a day of least expectation I hear that Jesus of Nazareth is passing by.[11]

Waiting by the wayside, like blind Bartimaeus, is an act of courage, of great faith even. Uncertain of immediate help and unsure of the final outcome, he knew only one thing. He had to be there, waiting patiently for God.

The Silence of God
Conclusion

To speak in such a way about God that he is hidden, elusive, ignored but not quite forgotten, enmeshed in the commonplace, the one for whom others must wait patiently, leads us towards one of the greatest of all discoveries about him. We become aware that amidst all the hectic doing and saying we are also receivers, for there is a 'givenness' in life.

The American poet, Wallace Stevens, writes of the occasions when we are given insights which we have not foreseen and for which we have not worked. They are not our achievements and can come upon us at any time:

> Perhaps
> The truth depends on a walk around a lake,
>
> A composing as the body tires, a stop
> To see hepatica, a stop to watch
> A definition growing certain and
>
> A wait within that certainty, a rest
> In the swags of pine-trees bordering the lake.
> Perhaps there are times of inherent excellence,
>
> As when the cock crows on the left and all
> Is well, incalculable balances,
> At which a kind of Swiss perfection comes
>
> And a familiar music of the machine
> Sets up its Schwärmerei, not balances
> That we achieve but balances that happen. . . .
>
> Perhaps there are moments of awakening,
> Extreme, fortuitous, personal, in which

The Opening Door

> We more than awaken, sit on the edge of sleep,
> As on an elevation, and behold
> The academies like structures in a mist.[12]

These 'balances that happen' should not be thought of as belonging exclusively to those who are committed to one religion or another. They are not the property of the faithful. They are common property because they speak of a God who is buried in commonplace things. How many rich experiences does life grant to us – the smile on the face of a sleeping child, the glance of friendship, the piece of music marvellously played or gloriously remembered – when in such 'moments of awakening' we realize that we are not far from the Kingdom of God.

2 *The Ambiguity of God*

Ambiguity is the last thing we expect from God. If he is any kind of God at all, we expect him to be decisive, clear and in control. Yet experience seems to indicate that such a god will at worst be a tyrant, and at best a haunting impossibility. Likewise, history shows that human beings who lay claim to the whole of God and who usually go on to lay claim to the whole of our allegiance as well are always false prophets. Despite all claims to the contrary, a measure of uncertainty is built into our experience of God, an uncertainty that stems just as much from God himself as from our human limitations in knowing him. It is said that a devil appeared to one of the Desert Fathers, those fourth-century Christians who sought God in the solitude of the wilderness. The devil appeared, however, as an angel of light and claimed to be the Angel Gabriel. The brother replied, 'Think again – you must have been sent to somebody else. I haven't done anything to deserve an angel!'[1]

The question then becomes one of recognition. Where do we look for him and what are the marks of his presence? In order to find ways of answering these questions, I find

The Opening Door

that I need to look at the biblical record and, in particular, at the stories told about Jesus after the resurrection.

Christians have sometimes given the impression that the Bible is the supreme argument-clincher. Biblical references are quoted rather like the playing of a trump card which settles the matter. Anyone who is outside the circle of faith, and an increasing number within it, finds this a difficult argument to accept and probably feels that those who use the Bible in this way are evading hard issues, stepping back from reality.

The Bible is not a retreat from reality, however, but rather an illumination of it. It holds a candle against the wind and throws a new light on our experience if we use it wisely. Our sense of its importance grows as our understanding of it grows. The more light it casts for us, the more we are prepared to say that it is a special book, but not one which is above criticism in the best sense of that word. Three stories, closely grouped together, have produced for me a quite vivid burst of light as I seek to answer the question, 'Can we recognize God in our experience and, if so, are there any clues to help us?'

(a) A case of mistaken identity

The writers who make us most aware of the importance, as well as the difficulty, of recognizing the presence of Christ are St John and St Luke. They tell three stories of how disciples who were intimately connected with Jesus failed to realize that they were in his presence after the resurrection. First there was Mary who wandered away from the empty tomb and encountered someone whom she took to be the gardener (John 20.15). She recognized him as he spoke her name 'Mary!'

The Ambiguity of God

Later that day, if we follow the general timing of the gospels, two disciples were wandering back rather disconsolately from Jerusalem to Emmaus talking about the crucifixion and the woman's tale of the empty tomb: 'As they talked and discussed it with one another, Jesus himself came up and walked along with them; but something kept them from seeing who it was' (Luke 24.15–16). They only recognized him when they had supper together in the evening and he broke the bread.

The third story occurred several days or weeks later. Seven disciples, including Simon Peter, went fishing. At dawn, says St John, 'there stood Jesus on the beach, but the disciples did not know that it was Jesus' (John 21.4).

All sorts of reasons are given why the disciples did not recognize the risen Lord. Mary was grief-stricken, her eyes filled with tears; the disciples were going westwards to Emmaus, their eyes blinded with the setting sun; it was dawn by the sea of Galilee and the fishermen were tired. But no matter how we try to explain these stories away, it has to be acknowledged that there are three of them in a comparatively short narrative about the resurrection, each one of them underlining the fact that Jesus was at first unrecognized. St Luke and St John really seem to be trying to tell us something about the essential nature of the resurrection. The disciples, men and women who had spent three years in close companionship with Jesus, who would have known every feature of his face, every intonation of his voice, every characteristic of his bearing, failed to realize that they were in his presence. Certain 'triggers' were needed – the personal name, the meal, the catch of fish – before it occurred to them that it was the risen Lord. This lack of immediate recognition seems to argue that the way in which Jesus was with his disciples was far from

The Opening Door

self-evident. Some special circumstances were needed for the 'penny to drop'. At best, the risen presence of Christ was ambiguous.

My suspicion, and it can only be a suspicion, is that in the days following the crucifixion, the disciples were asking questions about their experience with Jesus and, either individually or with others, they began to understand that the power and presence of Jesus lived on. This was not a constant experience. Some days there would be nothing; most days, in fact, there would be nothing; but every now and then, and always beyond their wildest expectations, it would dawn upon them that Christ was there with them, he was 'alive'. It was not just that his influence lived on in them. They were learning to 'see' with the eyes of faith. There was an excitement about it that was precious close to how it was when they were physically in his presence. For them, the whole experience of Christ, and by implication God, was becoming more profound.

Ordinary events and circumstances, which before were simply accepted and commonplace, became charged with greater meaning because 'Christ was there'. In one sense, you could say that the disciples' faith brought a new meaning to events; they saw things differently because they had been with Jesus. But this does not entirely do justice to the 'givenness' of their experiences of the risen Christ. The gospel writers, as they tell the stories of resurrection, seem to indicate that something was happening *to* the disciples, something which was independent of them, something which is symbolized by the empty tomb and the bodily presence of Jesus amongst them. My belief is that the first disciples, in their awareness of resurrection, were discovering that certain experiences have their own internal logic which is not easily

The Ambiguity of God

understood but which is disclosed as a gift if we are prepared to receive it.

As they shared their experiences of the 'livingness' of Christ, it would only be natural that they would try to connect up what they were going through then with what Jesus had said to them while he was still alive. What had he said about the presence of God in life? How had he promised to be with them? What was special, for instance, about the meal at Emmaus in which the two unsuspecting disciples had recognized him? They would have remembered other meals when important things had happened, meals for large crowds in Galilee, meals by dusty roads camping outside towns and villages when they scarcely had enough to go round, and one very special meal in an upper room the night he was betrayed. They would have remembered the distinctive way he took the bread, raised it to heaven in thanksgiving, broke it and shared it round, so distinctive in fact that the gospel writers refer to it time and time again in different stories. Their meals became a special focus of fellowship, particularly that meal, the bread and wine, of which Jesus had said, 'This is my body; this is my blood,' and that fellowship deepened into an awareness of the presence of God.

They would have become increasingly conscious of the importance of being together. Whether it was in the Upper Room, or in the companionship of a day's fishing in Galilee, there was something about being in each other's company that spoke to them about the companionship of Christ and which was crystallized for them in the saying of Jesus, '. . . where two or three have met together in my name, I am there among them' (Matt. 18.20). As they began to widen their horizons, and take their gospel to a larger and more hostile audience, they discovered another aspect of the risen

The Opening Door

presence of Christ, one which St Matthew captured in the final words of his gospel, 'Go forth therefore and make all nations my disciples... And be assured, I am with you always, to the end of time' (Matt. 28.20).

What I have been trying to do is to give an impression of resurrection faith which does not depend upon the literalness with which we are prepared to approach the gospel narrative of the empty tomb and the bodily appearances of Jesus. It is precisely the disciples' lack of certainty about his presence with them and their growing understanding of what it meant, which can most help us today, where our experience does not often embrace empty tombs and angels but where, nevertheless, there is something of the light of his presence. If we, too, fail to recognize him, we are doing no less than they; if we are to discover the signs of his glory, to touch the hem of his garment, then we must learn from their experience. Their discovery was that Christ was present in their meals, their being together, their relationships, their understanding of themselves, their awareness of others, their attempts to go to the limits of human experience to discover more truth and to share the light they had. Whether or not we are prepared to recognize him there depends upon our willingness to associate such commonplace things with God. It is the dilemma of a certain man called Nathanael, who, when they told him about Jesus, remarked rather doubtfully, 'Can anything good come from Nazareth?' (John 1.46).

(b) Power

One way of illustrating the ambiguity of God is to look at the language of power. The normal presentation of the life and ministry of Jesus runs something like this: the all-powerful

The Ambiguity of God

God, in his love for the world, restricted himself for thirty-three years to the ordinary humanity of Jesus of Nazareth; in Jesus we see restrained power at work, offering divine forgiveness but content to be ignored and happy ultimately to be rejected and even crucified by the very people he came to love and save. He is the picture of spurned love, quite literally 'a man of sorrows and acquainted with grief'.

But even as we follow through the story in our mind's eye, at the very moment when we rehearse the tale during Holy Week, we smile knowingly to ourselves: 'It's all right', we say, 'God will reassert himself, Jesus will return to the right hand of power; after all, God is still in charge.'

We have played a subtle form of the power game for we have modelled God on the idea of the monarch sitting on his throne, rewarding and punishing, answering petitions in an all-powerful, all-wise way, but, just once in a while, disguising himself as one of his subjects to find out what they are thinking.

This is of course a caricature and the reality of our presentation is much more profound and sensitive. However, the fact remains that we generally suppose God to be an all-seeing figure who can do what he likes but normally chooses not to. This is expressed in the answer often given to the puzzling state of affairs when devout people have prayed for healing without success: 'Well, I believe God could heal but either he chooses not to or our faith is not strong enough.'

None of this is mere theological word-spinning, for, like Nathanael, our expectations of God will control our appreciation of those moments when we recognize his presence. Nathanael, because of his preconceived ideas about what the Messiah should be, had to be convinced that Nazareth could be his home town. We, too, nurtured as we are on ideas of divine powerfulness, will have grave difficulty in recognizing

The Opening Door

the presence of God in similar commonplace things.

True enough, there are aspects of Jesus' teaching which appear to reflect God as a king, but we need to ask, 'What sort of king?' The overwhelming impression is of a God who is not powerful in the world's sense of being powerful. He is content to be misjudged, ignored, open to question. He does not always want the last word. On the contrary, gentleness becomes a virtue and service the touchstone of true greatness. God is apparently happy to hide himself in humanity, not as a temporary disguise, but as a permanent disclosure. One would have thought that this was the best kind of gospel or good news imaginable, but we, laden as we are with our own desire to be in charge, if only in a limited way, find it hard to accept. A. N. Whitehead has beautifully expressed the tragedy of it:

> The brief Galilean vision of humility flickered throughout the ages, uncertainly ... but the deeper idolatry of the fashioning of God in the image of the Egyptian, Persian and Roman imperial rulers, was retained. The church gave unto God the attributes which belonged exclusively to Caesar.[2]

It is this all-powerful God whom we invoke in our prayers in times of stress to be on our side; he holds the rod with which we can beat our enemies; his is the authority to which we will humbly submit to the point of negation of all that we are; it is to him that we turn to justify our ideas. It is this God who, as we say, 'uses' people, and we rarely pause to ask what it would imply if we said of another human being, 'Oh, he uses people.' Finally, it is from him that not a few will turn in disgust or disillusionment. For it is he who does nothing about undeserved suffering; it is he who enslaves not just those who offer themselves to him willingly but those many who are

The Ambiguity of God

enthralled by the few who know the tricks of the religious trade and use them to preserve worldly power and privilege. Ultimately it will be found that such a God is not just absent but that he never had the ability to be present except in the most harmful way.

But still we cling to him, as Marx and Freud and all the rest said we would, and the still, small voice of the stranger goes unheard.

One of the most liberating of all religious discoveries is the realization that God is not powerful in any recognizable, human way, indeed, that he cannot do everything. This realization frees us from the burden of defending the indefensible; it releases the anxiety of failure and the natural anger we feel at an unresponsive God; it lifts the burden of unrealistic expectations and it frees us for a deeper understanding of the presence of God. Writing of St Paul's growing awareness of the power and presence of God in his life through his own human frailty, Frederick Houk Borsch writes:

> Jesus on the cross and Paul with his recalcitrant Corinthians and thorn in the flesh found themselves in relationship with a God who did not intervene. He was visibly absent in the world; yet they found him to be invisibly present. He did not stand aloof but participated with them in their sufferings, and, in so doing, helped them to transform their meaning.[3]

The time in our lives when we become most aware of the presence or absence of God is the time of suffering. It is then that we begin either to appreciate the true power of God or to have doubts about it, and the way we eventually come to understand the power of God will determine whether or not we understand him to be present in our lives.

The Opening Door

Harold S. Kushner in his book *When Bad Things Happen to Good People*[4] tells the story of his family's experience of suffering and how this affected his own understanding of God. He and his wife had been concerned about their son, Aaron, when he had stopped gaining weight at the age of eight months. After his first birthday, his hair had begun to fall out. Prominent doctors assured them, however, that although Aaron would grow to be very short he would be normal in every other way. When Aaron was about three, Kushner and his wife moved from New York to a suburb of Boston where he became rabbi of a local congregation. A local paediatrician was working on the problem of children's growth and they took Aaron to see him. Two months later, the paediatrician told Kushner and his wife that the child was suffering from progeria, 'rapid ageing'. Aaron, he said, would never grow much beyond three feet, he would have no hair on his body, would look like an old man and would die in his teens.

The book is the record of how this young Jewish rabbi and his wife came to terms with that news against the background of the Jewish belief that God blessed the good and punished the bad with suffering. Even if he, Harold Kushner, was guilty of some major sin, of which he was not aware, and thus deserved, in Jewish terms, to be punished, this could not possibly be so with a three-year-old lad. The book is also a pastoral record of people who came to the young rabbi for help in their own times of suffering and how he dealt with them; people whose businesses collapsed, whose relatives were overtaken by disease, whose children were killed in motoring accidents, all asking the same question, 'Why should God let this happen to me? Where is God in all this?'

The problem is one of classic simplicity to state. If God is all-wise and all-loving and, at the same time, is also

The Ambiguity of God

all-powerful, why does he allow people to die in accidents and why does he allow such terrible diseases as Aaron's progeria? Kushner's answer is to remove that part of the equation which says that God can do anything. There is a randomness about nature with which we all have to come to terms.

At the same time, God is not absent from the suffering which he cannot prevent. He gives strength and perseverance to overcome it. He moves people to share the burden, people like those who made Aaron a scaled-down tennis racquet or the children 'who overlooked his appearance and physical limitations to play stickball with him in the backyard and who wouldn't let him get away with anything special.'[5] It is God who inspires others to become doctors and nurses and work sacrificially to sustain life and alleviate pain, or medical researchers to look for causes and cures.

Harold Kushner asks finally:

Can you learn to love and forgive Him despite His limitations, as Job does, and as you once learned to forgive and love your parents even though they were not as wise, as strong, or as perfect as you needed them to be?

And if you can do these things will you be able to recognize that the ability to forgive and the ability to love are the weapons God has given us to enable us to live fully, bravely, and meaningfully in this less-than-perfect world?[6]

Those are brave questions to ask for any believer in God. He acknowledges the help that he has had from the Christian theologian Dorothee Soelle and her book *Suffering*[7] and says that it is Christianity which 'introduced the world to the idea of a God who suffers.'[8] Here, from the Christian point of view, he goes right to the heart of the matter, for the risen Christ of whom the first disciples gradually became aware bore the marks of the nails in his hands. He was indeed a suffering God revealed most decisively on a cross and yet even beyond the cross his presence was characterized by pain, limitation and a sharing in our common humanity. Kushner, the Jewish rabbi, is denied this insight which comes from the risen Christ but he apprehends it from another direction, his son's deformity and his people's greatest hour of darkness, the Holocaust.

(c) Ministry

How is the limitation and powerlessness of God transformed into a positive sign of his presence in the world? The answer is contained in one word, 'ministry'. Jesus himself said, 'For even the Son of Man did not come to be served but to serve' (Mark 10.45). The essence of ministry is service. Three years ago I took part in a clowning workshop with a group of students at a conference centre in the Shenandoah Valley. To begin with, the clown looked just like everybody else. He talked about his experiences of being a clown, how it made him look at people and situations differently and how sometimes the presence of someone dressed in funny clothes and with a clown's face enabled the people to see things differently. As he spoke he put on his clown's suit and grease-paint. The more clown-like he became, the less he spoke until he 'said' everything in mime. He began to involve us in his clowning until at last he invited us, about twenty people, to sit in two lines, side by side, down the middle of the hall. Each person then raised his or her arm nearest the person opposite so that it looked as if the two lines were supporting a huge, invisible log. At this point the clown ran round and round the hall, picking up speed as he went, and then came racing down the middle of the hall towards where we were sitting. It looked as

The Ambiguity of God

if he was going to jump right over us, but he came to a shuddering halt right at the feet of the first two people in the line, much to our relief. Then he did it again, round the hall several times and then he hurtled towards us . . . and this time he simply took off, almost flying over our heads . . . and we caught him with our outstretched hands.

Clowns are not clever people by worldly standards. Their wisdom often looks ridiculous or obvious. Similarly their power, such as it is, is total weakness. They are constantly knocked down but always get up afterwards, a quality recalling J. B. Phillips' translations of Paul's catalogue of trials and tribulations in his service of the gospel: '. . . we may be knocked down but we are never knocked out!' (II Cor. 4.9). Somehow their faces carry a tear and a smile. They are laughably vulnerable and laughingly irrepressible.

Was the clown in the Shenandoah Valley trying to show that if you make yourself vulnerable, if you trust yourself to others, to God even, then sometimes you will not be let down? Was he trying to show that weakness which is all trust has a knack of drawing strength from others? Do the obvious needs of clowns trying to fly lead others, sometimes against their better judgment (any of us could have broken an arm), to work together to save them?

The theme of the clown as the symbol of ministry is taken up by Henri Nouwen in his book, *Clowning in Rome*.[9] Writing about his stay in Rome, he says that what left an indelible impression upon him was not the dignity and solemnity of the Roman Catholic Church or the urban terrorism of the Red Brigade but the little people who, as it were, took part in the interludes between the great scenes of the play: a few students, a priest, a Medical Mission sister, young men and women ministering in personal ways to drunks, drop-outs, old women and the handicapped. These are the clowns in the Roman circus.

> Clowns are not in the center of the events. They appear between the great acts, tumble and fall, and make us smile again after the tensions created by the heroes we came to admire. The clowns don't have it together, they do not succeed in what they try, they are awkward, out of balance, and left-handed but ... they are on our side. We respond to them not with admiration but with sympathy, not with amazement but with understanding, not with tension but with a smile.[10]

It is all a question of style. The clown will sometimes try to emulate his more illustrious companions, the lion-tamers and the tight-rope walkers, but he does it without self-importance and when he fails, as he almost certainly will, he does it with a smile as if to say, 'There you are: it's not so hard to fail. I can live with it.' It is a way of telling us that there are more important things, things that have to do with the simple humanities of life.

Ministry, similarly, is about the simple humanities of life. It has its own style. True enough, there will be times when ministry, in God's name, will be to take on the powers that be, the planners, the organizers, the authorities, because injustice cries out to be put right. But simply to take on the powers that be and beat them at their own game is to be in danger of becoming like 'them' and losing the essential style of the clown.

It was this clownish quality of ministry with which St Paul had to come to terms. Time and again his correspondence, particularly with the Corinthians, betrays his own personal anguish, the opposition that he met not just from hostile Jews

The Ambiguity of God

or indifferent Greeks but from critical Christians. Yet it was through his weakness and because of his own thorn in the flesh which God had sent 'to keep me from being unduly elated' (II Cor. 12.7) that he came to a true appreciation of the style of ministry that most effectively represented the love and presence of God.

> ... we are the impostors who speak the truth, the unknown men whom all men know; dying we still live on; disciplined by suffering, we are not done to death; in our sorrows we have always cause for joy; poor ourselves, we bring wealth to many; penniless, we own the world (II Cor. 6.8–10).

This style of ministry, the style of the clown who points away from all the values which are normally held to be desirable to those which are usually discounted, finds its deepest resonance in the style of Jesus' own ministry, which deliberately turned away from any form of worldly power. Indeed this deliberate turning away from worldly power was so final that its most effective symbol was a cross. St Paul says, again to the Corinthians:

> Jews call for miracles, Greeks look for wisdom; but we proclaim Christ – Yes, Christ nailed to the cross; and though this is a stumbling-block to Jews and folly to Greeks, yet to those who have heard his call, Jews and Greeks alike, he is the power of God and the wisdom of God.
>
> Divine folly is wiser than the wisdom of man, and divine weakness stronger than man's strength (II Cor. 1.22–25).

The similarity between the style of the circus clown and the style of Jesus is not lost on the poet Elizabeth Jennings. Addressing the clown directly, she speaks of his simple courage and his vulnerability:

The Opening Door

Have they forgotten that it takes as much
Boldness to tumble, entertain and jest
When loneliness walks tightrope in your breast
And every joke is like a wild beast's touch? ...
Strangely you remind
Of Christ on the cross.
Is it the seeming surrender or the white face,
The acceptance of loss?
Or simply that you seem like one not fallen from grace...?[11]

The clown, then, becomes a witness of a strangely compelling kind, linking ministry, with its humanity and frailty, to a glimpse of the Other, to the God who gives of himself to the point of powerlessness and rejection.

How then is it possible to discern the unrecognized Christ in this style of ministry? The gospel story which speaks most strongly to many modern Christians, particularly the young, is the Parable of the Sheep and the Goats (Matt. 25.31-46). This is not to say that this will always be the case. Different generations perceive their own Christ and so it must always be. But many of this generation will find great stimulus in the words of Jesus: 'When I was hungry, you gave me food; when thirsty, you gave me drink; when I was a stranger you took me into your home, when naked you clothed me; when I was ill you came to my help, when in prison you visited me.' We need continually to remind ourselves of the force of the repeated 'me' just as we continually need reminding of the amazement of the so-called sheep, 'Lord, when was it that we saw you hungry and fed you, or thirsty and gave you drink...?'

Just as the disciples, in the days following the crucifixion, discovered the presence of the risen Christ in their being

The Ambiguity of God

together, in their meals, in their commonplace lives, so to their great astonishment they were to discover him in their ministry to 'my brothers here, however humble'. The Christ of their prayers and their meal-table was the Christ of their ministry to ordinary men and women. He was the same Christ, though often unrecognized and the better served for being so.

Mother Teresa says:

> In Holy Communion we have Christ under the appearance of bread. In our work we find him under the appearance of flesh and blood. It is the same Christ. 'I was hungry, I was naked, I was sick, I was homeless.'[12]

Christ, the unrecognized God, is present in ministry, in that style of selfless giving which points to other values. It would be presumptuous for any one group of people, believers or not, to claim that they alone recognize him. That is only to play another form of the power game, the rules for which include proving that 'my' light is brighter than 'yours'. Suffice it to say that many people discover in ministry a depth to experience which they never knew was there; it is an opening door between a world that is often a cul-de-sac of ambition and aggression and a world where the human spirit finds its true home in giving and receiving.

Make no mistake, receiving is just as important a part of ministry as giving. May I put the point in the form of a personal story. In the summer of 1976, my wife and I and our two children were visiting Gatlinberg, a resort town high up in the Smoky Mountains of East Tennessee. As we got out of the car on a hot, humid day, one of our daughters slammed the car-door shut on her thumb. Despite the heat and the pain she insisted that we carry on with our visit, but it soon became apparent that she was in great distress. We looked for a place to sit down and buy a Coke but the main street was crowded and there were no seats anywhere. Just as we were about to return to the car, we saw a motel with half a dozen chairs drawn up against a wall. We hurried over and our daughter sat down. Then we noticed a sign over the chairs which read, 'These chairs are reserved for motel guests only.' Within seconds, the motel door opened and out strode a burly woman who was quite obviously the receptionist. I hurriedly prepared my defence but I need not have worried. 'Your child looks ill,' she said. 'Would she like a glass of water?'

Perhaps it is not only in giving but also in receiving, in being in the position of weakness as well as the position of strength, that we minister Christ to one another and learn the secret of the cup of cold water given in his name. Like the cross, the cup of cold water is apparently a particularly inadequate symbol for God in the face of the enormous problems of the world, many of them beyond our control but equally, many the result of man's folly and penchant for power. Often it will be swept aside by the very forces to which it seeks to minister. Because it is offered by human hands, it will sometimes become tainted with self-interest. And yet, in the hands of a Mother Teresa or a Ghandi or an unknown woman in Gatlinberg it will be a powerful sign of God's presence. Embraced by a whole organization, like the Hospice movement or Oxfam or Christian Aid, it will become an effective symbol of the power of the Other to point to values which instinctively we know to be right. The Other need not be named. In his weakness he is content to go unrecognized, just as the villagers of Nazareth asked uncomprehendingly about Jesus, 'Is not this the carpenter?' (Mark 6.3).

The Ambiguity of God

Conclusion

Nathanael's dilemma, told by the fourth evangelist, was that he could not possibly see how the Messiah could come from Nazareth (John 1.43–51). Nathanael's expectations of how God should act were altogether grander.

We too have our expectations of God and those expectations will either illuminate or conceal him. My purpose has been to show that there is a strand in the biblical record, it is not the only strand, which points to the unrecognized God in human experience, unrecognized because he comes at us against all our expectations, from the position of weakness. He is not what we supposed. Rather than the fairy-tale prince who disguises himself as a pauper, but only for a while, he is in our experience the unknown, the hidden, the buried, the almost recognized.

3 *The Presence of God*

The recurring theme in our thinking about the experience of God is that of the opening door. But the door is not always open, as many of the great religious thinkers have found. There are times when God seems far away in his hiddenness, and times when we are far away from him in our frailty. The resurrection stories told by the gospel writers seem to indicate that this is not far from the true state of things, for the disciples were not always sure of the risen Christ. Their experience of him came and went, and surely an important part of the significance of the story of the Ascension is that they should learn that their lasting relationship with God was not to be a constant thing based on sight but the kind of in-and-out affair which rests upon faith.

God was still to be known, the door would remain open, but he had to be discovered in the midst of ordinary life and, as likely as not, would be elusive and fleeting. The poet R. S. Thomas has written of these elusive moments of discernment using the biblical ideas of the burning bush, the pearl of great price and the treasure buried in the field.

The Opening Door

> I have seen the sun break through
> to illuminate a small field
> for a while, and gone on my way
> and forgotten it. But that was the pearl
> of great price, the one field that had
> the treasure in it. I realize now
> that I must give all that I have
> to possess it. Life is not hurrying
> on to a receding future, nor hankering after
> an imagined past. It is the turning
> aside like Moses to the miracle
> of the lit bush, to a brightness
> that seemed as transitory as your youth
> once, but is the eternity that awaits you.[1]

But the poem, which is called *The Bright Field*, not only points out the fleeting quality of this experience of God, as fleeting as the momentary shaft of sunlight between the racing clouds, it indicates an understanding of who, or what, God is. There are moments in life which are worth having for their own sake, pointers to those things which we count as significant for us. Those moments jump out at us, they overtake us without warning. With time for reflection they may be woven into a seamless robe, but even one such moment may have an eternal value for us; it may change us for ever.

There are many 'Bright Fields' but here I would like to suggest just three: relationships, story, and 'limit situations'. Each one, I believe, is a contemporary experience of God and yet each one can be traced to the New Testament understanding of the presence of the risen Christ. In none of them is it at all easy to refer to God as 'he', to give him personality in any way that we would understand personality. But in each of

The Presence of God

them I grow increasingly conscious of the Other which I call God.

(a) God in relationships

In 1963 a group of students met in a college room in Cambridge with an eminent professor whose subject was the philosophy of religion. It was a year of more than usual interest and importance. John F. Kennedy had recently been assassinated; Bishop John Robinson had just published his radical book *Honest to God*. The full force of student protest was still to be felt but there were already straws in the wind.

There was no set topic for conversation but the talk turned in the direction of the ordained ministry for which the students were intended. The eminent professor recounted how one family he knew was helped by the visits of their pastor at a time of bereavement. 'What did he say?' inquired a friend. 'He didn't say anything,' came the reply, 'he simply sat and wept with us.' There was already a closeness in the group, but the story and its teller made the occasion more profound.

The point of maintaining that God is not always known as a person, of whom we will say 'He is present', is that it sometimes avoids unrealistic or plain wrong expectations. The group of students did not immediately begin looking over their shoulders rather uneasily, expecting to see some kind of spectral presence as the professor finished the story with tears in his eyes. Some of them, however, were aware that the conversation had imperceptibly engaged a higher gear. God was present, but not as a third party, 'outside' what was taking place in that college room. The personal pronoun, 'he', referring to God, might even have got in the way of recognizing that the bond of fellowship itself, as Christians traditionally describe it, was an experience of God.

It is really not surprising that if God is to be experienced anywhere at all, it will be through personal relationship. A. N. Whitehead may have been right when he said, 'Religion is what the individual does with his solitariness . . . and if you are never solitary, you are never religious.'[2] But that is not the whole truth. Our lives are comprised of relationships, some more profound than others, but all dependent upon the interplay of other minds and bodies with our own. Is it not reasonable to expect that we shall discover God in them?

An indication of the importance of relationships was given in a leading article in the British Medical Journal which discussed a case where a newly-born and badly handicapped child was apparently left to die, not from neglect, but because the paediatrician believed it was the kindest thing to do. Such a difficult ethical decision is forced upon doctors by the fact that virtually every infant weighing over 2000g. can now be kept alive.

> 'The effect', to quote Richard A. McCormick, a distinguished American Catholic moral theologian, 'is that the problem has been shifted to the quality of life sustained.' McCormick sees life as a relative, not an absolute, good and argues that life is a value to be preserved only in so far as it contains some potentiality for human relationships.[3]

This definition of the value of human life in terms of the possibility of relationships is almost certainly not absolute. It is, nonetheless, an interesting pointer to the deep underlying worth of human relationships. There are some people, of course, who lead solitary lives and are greatly fulfilled in their solitariness. However, the capacity for relationships remains

The Presence of God

and what they are now as human beings is what they became through their earlier experience of parents and others. In other words, Robinson Crusoe is always a possibility but Tarzan must ever remain a fiction.

In the magnificent poem of creation with which the Bible opens, the writer is giving significance, in his own terms, to what he sees around him. It is natural for him to say that all things have their origin in God, most of all mankind:

> Then God said, 'Let us make man
> in our own image and likeness . . .'
> So God created man in his own image;
> in the image of God, he created him;
> male and female, he created them (Gen. 1.26–27).

The author's way of writing poetry, in which the thought of one line is taken up and expanded in the next, perhaps indicates that for him the phrase 'the image of God' is explained by the possibility of relationships. God himself is spoken of in the plural, 'Let us make man in our image', while 'man' in the original Hebrew (Adam) did not indicate one individual but many. The divine image which is finally left upon mankind contains all the possibilities of relationship, 'male and female, he created them'. The relationship of one person with another is nothing less than a reflection of God who is the focal point of all relationships. Indeed, person-to-person relationships may not only be reflections of the image of God but participations in it. God is present in relationships.

There is abundant evidence to show that this was the experience of the apostles after the resurrection. The most startling story, already referred to, is that of the two disciples travelling to Emmaus after the Resurrection.

That same day two of them were on their way to a village

called Emmaus, which lay about seven miles from Jerusalem, and they were talking together about all these happenings. As they talked and discussed it with one another, Jesus himself came up and walked along with them; but something kept them from seeing who it was (Luke 24.13–35).

They recognized Jesus only as they ate supper with him at journey's end but their being together, their journey, their talk and their shared loss held the possibility of the presence of the risen Christ in the most vivid way. In the same way, it seems to have been important for the apostles to be together, probably in the Upper Room, for the risen Christ to make himself known (John 20.19–26) and for that most dramatic experience of the presence of God, the coming of the Holy Spirit at Pentecost (Acts 2.1). Indeed, as they stayed together so their understanding of God deepened (Acts 2.43–47).

Moreover, Bishop John Taylor has pointed out the twoness of the New Testament, Peter and John at the Beautiful Gate, Paul and Barnabas, Paul and Silas, Barnabas and Mark. He has also drawn our attention to the way in which the Greek word, *allelon*, 'one another', is used so often; wash one another's feet, serve one another, forbear and forgive one another, build one another up, bear one another's burdens, love one another. He writes: 'Like a peal of bells the word *allelon* – "one another" – rings through the pages of the New Testament.'[4]

Whatever the reality behind the apostles' experiences of being together, it seems that it was, for them, a most important medium by which to experience God. Not that it was, or is, an everyday occurrence, despite all our human contacts. Indeed, it would be hardly bearable always to be recognizing

The Presence of God

God in our midst in such a personal and poignant way. Special moments are given, however, which we ought neither to ignore nor despise.

'No, I don't know about God,' wrote someone who was asked how one talked about God; 'but let me be friends with Mick outside Simon House, or let me walk with my husband across Port Meadow at sunset, or let me sit in silence through someone else's family quarrel, and I can tell you a part of the joy and despair of God's *things* – and perhaps *that* can tell others something, however small, about Him; and what's more, I believe that the telling can be done without it being remote or belittling or trivializing, because that telling is not about God direct, but of His things here on earth which are ours too.'

The relationships which hold the promise of God are not necessarily the intensely loving, permanent relationships between two people who share each other's lives in marriage. No doubt, those relationships have their own kind of ecstasy and what is said of wider and less exclusive relationships will also be said of them. But being friends with 'Mick outside Simon House' holds the possibility of revealing God, just as does 'a walk with my husband across Port Meadow'. There may be two people or more than two. They may be in a permanent relationship or in an occasional, temporary one. Some people will recognize God in personal terms – 'He was there'. Others will be content simply to hold on to 'the intensity', 'the appropriateness' of the moment, calling it 'God' nonetheless in their heart of hearts.

What is it about relationships that holds the possibility of God? There may be no answer to that question. 'Be grateful for the experience and don't examine it too closely,' some will say. Others, however, will brush aside the whole idea of God

The Opening Door

and call it sheer emotionalism. For that reason, the question needs to be pressed as far as it will go. What is it that is so inherently good about a relationship that it has in it the possibility of revealing God?

A number of possibilities emerge although none of them fits every case. The first possibility is talk. Many people will have had the experience of talking with a friend or a group of friends and coming to the realization that more has been happening than simply having a good chat. Such talk often begins with unimportant things, things we have done that day, people we have met, or a conversation about a mutual friend. One particular subject seems to be more important and for the moment it becomes the centre of the talk. If there is time, if the friends feel secure enough in each other's company, other subjects for talk emerge, an anxiety, a doubt, a cause for joy, an ambition, a failure. Such a relationship between friends, achieved through talk, is an ever-deepening event. Layer by layer, the defences are thrown down until one of them feels secure enough to say something which ordinarily would remain unsaid. This gesture of confidence calls forth a response from the others and the talk slowly becomes more deeply personal. It is as if each is making himself or herself vulnerable in the presence of the others, entrusting to words those things which in the cold light of day would seem impossibly dangerous and threatening. The end of the talk is unpredictable but each knows when that end has come. Sometimes the conversation will suddenly become altogether lighter as if they cannot bear too much. Sometimes the conversation is stilled completely and all that remains is a pool of silence.

It is in the very vulnerability which the talk of friends both encourages and embodies that God is found. In it, two or

The Presence of God

three become one for a moment, discovering the common bond between them, the bond which is God.

A second possibility is the mutual giving and receiving of worth and dignity, a recognition of shared humanity. This seems to have been the point of the philosopher's story within the story with which this chapter began. No words were spoken in the moment of bereavement, just the weeping of the pastor with its recognition of the intensity of another's grief.

It is one of the truisms of our times that we treat people as 'things' unless we are very careful not to. They happen to be there on the bus, at the cash till, behind the wheel, on the other end of the telephone, on the screen. The vast majority of people are not people in their own right as far as we are concerned. They are simply part of the furniture of our world. How else could we do things that hurt others so much? It takes an enormous effort of the imagination for them to be otherwise. Of all the people who inhabit our world there are a certain number with whom we deal as human beings, mostly because we speak to them. And of these, only a relative handful seem to us persons in their own right, as we know ourselves to be.

We know that we ourselves are persons. Behind the mask which is our face, there is a whole country of feelings, skills, fears, joys, friendships, animosities, hopes, ideals. We call it our personality. Because there are one or two others whom we know well, we realize that there must be other persons like us. After all, we are not the centre of the world, there are others there too. It seems doubtful that we are all at the same centre with the same world spinning around us all. More likely we are each at the centre of our own individual but overlapping worlds.

From time to time, another human being is thrust into our

world and asks to be taken seriously as a person, demanding our time, our patience, our energies, our recognition. 'It's asking a lot,' we say to ourselves, 'I can't afford too much recognition. My world is only big enough for my wife, my children and a few close friends. I haven't the emotional energy, the time to cope with any more *persons*.' However, if we allow ourselves to be imposed upon, hand out a little more recognition, embrace another person into our world, we may find to our surprise that the other person may not only take but give and in that mutuality of recognition there is the possibility of God.

Talk and recognition are two possible answers to the question, 'Where is God in relationships?' There may well be other more satisfactory ones. However, in Christianity love is seen as the authentic expression of that which is ultimate and since love is rarely solitary, it must be seen in the context of a relationship. Let it be emphasized that the relationship is not necessarily one of those profound, long-lasting relationships. There are many kinds of relationships envisaged by the commandment, 'Love your neighbour.' What matters is the quality of the love. It is not exclusive, Christ's love, the life force that leads to fear because it is based on a jealous desire to keep what we have. Christianity affirms that love is inclusive, as John Wren Lewis has written,

> . . . that openness to real love leads every pair of friends or lovers to go out beyond themselves and include more and more third persons in their relationships just as the descent of the Holy Spirit in power on the day of Pentecost drove the group of friends of Jesus to 'go into all the world' and strive to bring all the world into their relationship. Exclusivity, Christianity asserts, is a denial of an essential activity

of love and therefore of love itself, for there are not three Gods but one God and it is because this denial takes place, all over the world, that aggressive forces are generated in people. That is why fallen society is based on fear, as Freud saw, but in a society that is really human and not made inhuman by denial of love, social relations will be 'rooted and grounded in love'.[5]

The unknown visionary of the first chapter of Genesis knew that men and women were made in the image of God. He knew too that the giving, accepting and overflowing of human love that is implied in any human relationship worthy of the name, is a sharing in the ultimate relationship of the God who is mysteriously Father, Son and Spirit.

(b) God the story

When the writer Colin Welland received his Oscar in 1982 for the screenplay of the film *Chariots of Fire* he was asked to what he attributed the film's success. He said that when he saw the film for the first time the audience had remained seated at the end, quite still. It was as if the film had spoken to some half-forgotten spiritual side in all of them.

The film told the story of the preparations of two very different British runners, Abrahams and Liddell, for the 1924 Olympic Games in Paris and in fact had a very 'religious' subplot. Eric Liddell the young Scottish preacher destined to be a missionary in China, who would not run on the Sabbath even in the Olympics; Harold Abrahams the young Jewish student struggling with charges of professionalism and Cambridge anti-Semitism; both in the end victorious in their different ways.

The Opening Door

We do not need to be reminded of the importance of stories, whether they are told in the time-honoured way of the story-teller or in the technicoloured medium of the film-maker. Cinema-going may not be as popular as once it was, but whole generations have been captivated by the great 'film myth'. 'It's only entertainment,' we say, but it is entertainment founded upon compelling principles of human activity; that of living exciting dramas through heroes, that of achieving self-forgetting, even for an hour, when there is much or, perhaps even worse, little to be forgotten. Whether we read a good story or watch it we are 'absorbed', we exchange our 'story' for the one that is offered to us. Momentarily, it will be better than ours, especially if it has a good ending. Mostly, we return to reality when the story finishes. No harm has been done. Nothing has changed as we blink our way out of the cinema into the cold light of day. It has been good fun, sheer entertainment.

Occasionally we find in a curious way that the two stories meet, that which is ours and that which is the teller's or the writer's. Perhaps they have a common setting, we recognize a character, part of the plot is familiar, or we feel we have been there. Something speaks to us, as obviously it did to those who watched *Chariots of Fire*.

Professor Ian Ramsey has described certain experiences as 'disclosures'. They 'disclose' something important to us, something which may not be apparent superficially but which lies hidden, waiting almost for the right moment. Certain phrases are used in everyday speech to describe what is happening. Of these, Ian Ramsey writes:

Such phrases, for example, as those which speak of situations 'coming alive', 'taking on depth', situations in which

The Presence of God

the 'penny drops', where 'we see' but not with the eyes of flesh, where something 'strikes us', where 'eye meets eye' and where 'hearts miss a beat'. Such situations may be of a dramatic and spectacular kind to which a metaphor like 'the ice breaks' is plainly appropriate, or they may be of the kind where we gradually come to 'see' so that we speak more appropriately of 'the light dawning'.[6]

What Ian Ramsey believed, and indeed tried to show, was that there are in life, situations which disclose God in such a way. The possibilities are endless but here I am seeking to relate Ian Ramsey's 'disclosures' to what happens sometimes when we are confronted by a story.

It may sound a little unusual to talk about our 'story' as if we were characters in a novel. But it may not be so wide of the mark. With a little reflection, it is possible to perceive that our lives are shaped like stories. Not only do they have beginnings, middles and ends, but they have moments of high drama when decisions have to be made and when our lives interlock with others to produce tension, sadness, opportunity or joy. A friend of mine once told me that there was a dramatic moment in her life when she had to make a conscious decision to work as a nurse in a certain Chicago hospital, or leave town and find a new career. She stayed, took the job and as a consequence, which she had no way of foreseeing, met her husband who was also working there. That was a moment of drama which radically affected her life, and the life of her future husband. It is the sort of drama which scores of authors have written about.

We recall our past, as that person did for me the afternoon we spoke, or as a person will do as they tell you about 'their war', in the form of a narrative. Our memory does not usually

The Opening Door

produce a tedious catalogue of happenings but rather the 'edited' highlights. The boring bits are not recalled; sometimes the painful passages are cut; often our memories play tricks so that events run together, get in the wrong order. But by the peculiar facility of memory the events fit together into a story which helps us make sense of what we have done, who we are and how we come to be where we are now.

Is the future story-shaped? Does the narrative that we impose upon our past stretch into our future? The future is, of course, open to a large extent. It would be a bleak prospect indeed if it were not. However, the future becomes available to us through our imagination. In order to make decisions in the present, or simply to while away the time in our daydreams, we devise stories about our futures, scenarios as they are now called, in which we become principal characters and in which various story-lines are tried out. We do not always abandon our future story when the time for action comes; if we have marked out our future, if we know where we are going, we might well decide to stick to it come what may. It is the stuff of ambition.

Lying behind the stories of our own lives, the stories we tell about ourselves and about our world, there is what I want to call the Big Story. The Big Story is just beyond the best work of the serious novelist or film-maker although they participate in it. The Big Story is approached through a succession of words – tale, fable, legend, saga, epic, myth. These may be stories of long ago, of the present or indeed of the future. They tell of how things were intended to be, of how things might still be with luck or something more than luck. They themselves are not the Big Story, for that is never told in so many words, only hinted at. It has to do with how we see ourselves as human beings distinct from the rest of the world, with how

The Presence of God

we organize our values, with how we cope with human frailty and death. The Big Story is about time and hope and most frequently has tragic overtones. The Big Story is never simply narrated, it is celebrated or it is mourned. Or, to change the metaphor, it is lived in, like an old dwelling-place.

When a story which is told overlaps with our own story at some critical point there is the likelihood of an intuitive appreciation of our place within the Big Story. The penny drops, we see in a more profound way. It is this point of disclosure that I would wish to associate with God; not God as he is normally talked about, but as the unexpected depth beyond depth within each of us, to which the writer Colin Welland referred in his own way. Stories, some more than others, have the capacity to stir within us half-forgotten abilities and hopes. They can remind us both of human grandeur and human degradation. Story is matched only by music in its ability to inspire vision and action, and when the two come together as one they stir human imagination as few things can.

In all this, it should come as no surprise that at the heart of the Christian story, there is a story-teller. Some of his stories are extremely brief, one-liners about grains of wheat, mustard seed and lumps of salt and leaven. In them he is not so much concerned to tell a story as to set the scene, to put out a signpost for us by using words in unfamiliar ways. 'You are the light of the world. A city set on a hill cannot be hid' (Matt. 5.14). 'Use your imagination' he says to us and as we do so we find we are beginning to place ourselves within a story of sorts.

At the other end of the scale, there are full-blown parables, memorable and beautifully rounded stories, some of which, like the Good Samaritan and the Prodigal Son, have passed into literary history and become part of common speech. Our

The Opening Door

problem with stories such as these is that we have become comfortable in them. We miss their vigour, their sheer impertinence, because we have heard them often. We have been taught to understand them merely as illustrations in an otherwise difficult sermon, as quiet resting-places in a demanding journey of the spirit. Nothing could be further from the truth.

The challenge of the parable has long been felt. Fifty years ago, the New Testament scholar T. W. Manson wrote: 'It is not a crutch for limping intellects, but a spur to religious insight; its object is not to provide simple theological instruction, but to produce living religious faith.'[7]

In the last decade scholars have looked ever more closely at the form and structure of New Testament literature but Manson's verdict remains fundamentally unchanged. The stories of Jesus are not easy extensions of his more difficult teaching. They are themselves difficult, awkward rather than easy to handle, often opaque rather than transparent, active and wriggling from our grasp like so many eels rather than comfortable sermon illustrations. Jesus' stories frequently, if not always, invite us to take part in them; they overlap at all sorts of unexpected points with our own stories. The trick is not so much our interpretation of the parables but how they will interpret us. The parable of the Good Samaritan (Luke 10.25–37) ends with the most awkward of questions which does not quite match up with the question that first inspired the story, 'Who is my neighbour?' but we, no more than the persistent lawyer, cannot avoid the challenging word of Jesus the story-teller.

But that is not all. For the genius of Jesus' stories lies not just in the compelling questions that they ask but also in the way he had of taking material that was already to hand, casting what was commonplace, familiar and ordinary in a new mould. What was Jesus implying about God when he told tales about rich men trying, unsuccessfully, to give parties for their friends, or building bigger and better barns, or ignoring the claims of the poor at their gate? Was he saying, 'God is like this, only more so', or simply and most challengingly, 'God is like this'?

Sally McFague sees the importance of the familiarity of Jesus' stories:

> The parables again and again indicate that it is in the seemingly insignificant events of being invited to a party and refusing to go, being jealous of a younger brother who seems to have it all his own way, resenting other workers who get the same pay for less work, that the ultimate questions of life are decided.[8]

Of course, it was no accident that the stuff of Jesus' stories is everyday life. The natural tenor of his life was not to indicate a God who had intervened in human life from the outside, but to draw attention to the God who was already deep down in life itself. His God, whom he calls Father, is part of the warp and woof of everyday existence and, once perceived, drastically alters our attitudes, our perspective, our sense of direction. Or, to put it another way, Jesus' intention was not to bring down some theological blueprint from on high, a plan for mankind which was unendingly true but unendingly dull. Rather was it to draw out of us in a living way that which is already there and characteristic of the highest and the best of which human experience is capable. His truest insight was that this could be done in two ways, to tell stories and to embody them in all that he was, and thus to provoke the response. His story-telling, because it resonates so frequently with the Big Story and because it is so ordinary and overlaps

The Opening Door

with our story at so many points, is full of the possibilities of disclosing God if we have a mind to listen.

I have written at some length about the stories of Jesus because they are not incidental to his ministry, the icing on the theological cake. They are much more important than that. They *are* his ministry to a much greater extent than we have normally allowed and we must reckon with this in the perspective of the importance of all stories for us. Furthermore, it is not only Jesus' stories which can reveal God. Other stories, not necessarily 'religious' can do the same. My point is that when a story resonates, as we say, or when light dawns, or the penny drops, then we are experiencing something of great significance. The Big Story is being heard from afar and although the experience may be no clearer than that, it is nevertheless an echo of what is eternally true and what is true for us in that particular moment.

The stories which can do this for us are many. They may be fable or legend, fiction or biography. They may be serious and tragic or they may be humorous; most certainly they will be humorous. They may be 'religious', in whatever sense we can give to that word, or they may be secular or worldly. I would not like to judge between Lear and Job, except to say that Job is a bench-mark of sorts, indicating a truth about God which has to be included in any picture of him.

Evelyn Waugh's *Brideshead Revisited* is criticized by some for being too full of a sentimental kind of Catholicism and by others as less than Waugh's stylistic best. But recently it was televised very successfully with story and music in a superb combination. The book tells of the unexpected return of Charles Ryder to the once-magnificent country house of Brideshead. He comes now as an Army Captain in charge of his Company, with orders to make the place suitable for

The Presence of God

billeting. His revisit conjures up his past ambiguous relationship with the Marchmains, an old Catholic family, who one by one reject the faith of their mother but curiously find their own way to God.

There is a strong sense of decay running throughout the book, of which the old house is the symbol. Once full of life and finery, now run-down, knocked about, deserted except for soldiers who might as well belong to a different age. And yet, the army being what it is, the soldiers have their chaplain, and the old chapel, long forsaken, has been brought back into use and the altar-lamp relit.

At first, it seemed to Charles Ryder that all the centuries of building the great house had come to nothing in what he crushingly calls 'the age of Hooper', his graceless adjutant. 'Vanity of vanities, all is vanity,' he is tempted to say.

> And yet, I thought, and yet that is not the last word, it is not even an apt word; it is a dead word from ten years back.
>
> Something quite remote from anything the builders intended, has come out of their work, and out of the fierce little human tragedy in which I played; something none of us thought about at the time; a small red flame – a beaten copper lamp of deplorable design relit which the old knights saw from their tombs, which they saw put out; that flame burns again for other soldiers, far from home, further, in heart, than Acre or Jerusalem.
>
> It could not have been lit but for the builders and the tragedians, and there I found it this morning, burning anew among the old stones.[9]

For Charles Ryder, it was a moment of seeing, as it is perhaps for the reader or the watcher. At that point, faith is more than morality, transcending credal formulation and assent.

The Opening Door

It is a way of seeing and being seen, an experience of God. Like St Paul, we see only partially, through a glass darkly, but we press on seeking to understand, looking for light in the darkness, confident that one day we shall see face to face and know as we are known.

(c) God at the limits

One morning a girl named Jenny called to see me. She had come at the suggestion of a friend. At first she was almost struck dumb. The effort showed on her face as she struggled to find words to express thoughts which lay deep beneath the surface, thoughts that obviously caused her the utmost pain. Finally she blurted out her agony, 'It's so unfair. I've tried every approach to God I can think of but without success. Does God choose who he wants to believe in him?'

Jenny was at the limits of her humanity. She was like the mime artist trapped against the invisible wall of glass, trying desperately to find a way through. At the limits, at the outer edges of her humanity she was touching the outer edges of what we call God, unsuccessfully as it seemed to her.

Being at the limits is a common human experience and because these experiences are often associated with sadness and pain we regard them as undesirable – with justification. And yet, it is often in the ultimate situations that we are most ourselves. We test our resources. We find out what we are made of and even in failure, perhaps most of all in failure and being all at sea, we discover what it means to be human beings.

It has been the experience of some people that being in a particular limit situation has not only put them in touch with themselves but has put them in touch with God also. The

The Presence of God

German theologian, Jürgen Moltmann, tells of how he spent three years as a prisoner of war of the British after 1945. Not only did he have to cope with the defeat of his country but also the guilty revelation of the crimes of Buchenwald and the other camps. His inner world was threatened with collapse and would have been destroyed utterly but for the fact that the humiliation and forsakenness gradually became an experience of God. He discovered in the Psalms that God was present with those 'that are of a broken heart' and as he prowled the perimeter fence he found that his thoughts of freedom turned towards the small hut that served as a chapel in the centre of the camp. He writes:

> God in the night of the soul – God as the power of hope and pain: this was the experience which moulded me in what are a person's most receptive years, between 18 and 21. I am reluctant to say that this is why I became a Christian, because that sounds like joining a party. Because I believe that I owe my survival to these experiences, I cannot even say I found God there. But I do know in my heart that it is there that he found me, and that I would otherwise have been lost.[10]

In limit situations the verdict can always go two ways. Indeed the experience of God which the ultimate produces would have no validity were it not possible for the same set of circumstances to lead to exactly the opposite conclusion. This is in fact what Moltmann argues repeatedly in his book *The Crucified God*. The ministry of Jesus with its in-built high risk factor of being rejected totally is the key to God's true identity. If, in the ultimate situations of life, men and women reject God, they are doing no more than carrying to its ultimate

The Opening Door

conclusion the cry of the crucified One, 'My God, my God, why hast thou forsaken me?' (Mark 15.34).

The experience of being a prisoner of war is an unusual example of a limit situation. There are other examples much closer to hand. Birth, illness, marriage, divorce, bereavement are all about human beings touching the outer edges of their humanity. These are the common experiences. No single human being is untouched by some combination of them. Indeed, the sociologist Emile Durkheim believed that religion came into being not as a response to invisible powers and capricious gods but as a way of enabling human beings to cope with the ultimate mysteries of living, bringing to birth and dying.

Sadly some churches turn their back upon men and women who are at the limits. This is most typically seen in attitudes to divorced people who wish to remarry. But there is also a growing practice of seeking to outlaw what is sometimes called 'indiscriminate baptism', the baptism of children whether or not their parents are practising Christians. This is done by insisting on some form of qualification. In reality the result is the very opposite of what baptism means, stressing as it does, our inadequacy, our lack of preparation and the sheer generosity of a giving God who is prepared to risk rejection. The practical consequences of turning away people who are at the limits is to imply that the particular experience through which they are going, which for some is the most important thing that has ever happened to them, has nothing to do with God. But their need is often the very opposite of this. That is the very time when people need symbols, ways of interpreting what is happening to them, and help with weaving the experience into the pattern of their lives.

'It's only right to have it in church' may seem to the priest a rather inadequate reason for surrounding one's important occasion with religious sounds and symbols, but, given the reluctance and the inability of the average person to talk about spiritual things, it is not theologically inarticulate. They may well be saying, as the cynics suggest, that what they want is a nice setting for the photographs. But they may also be saying that they wish to affirm a half-realized, part-forgotten spiritual side to their human nature called God. If the church refuses to take the risk, refuses to be open to the real possibilities of any human relationship, particularly in the way I talked about relationship in an earlier chapter, we are really saying that men and women have to qualify for God much as they would have to do for a tennis tournament. We need not be surprised if people take their 'buried life' elsewhere, or allow it to remain buried.

People at the limits, in a wide variety of circumstances, will 'use' the church, or appear to. They will not always return or be grateful, although often they are. They may give every appearance of taking it lightly, of not treating the matter with the seriousness we feel it deserves. But does the doctor or the lawyer expect all his clients to return? Do you expect the plumber to call in every week to inspect the plumbing job he did for you recently? In a world increasingly full of what we like to call 'service industries' the fact that a service is called upon only infrequently does not diminish its value. People have long memories for the places where they were treated as human beings, where their needs were taken seriously and where they were not asked for that which was beyond their capabilities to give.

Will we put restrictions upon our 'service'? When people at the limits reach out and touch the outer edges of God in their very humanity, perceiving their own opening doors,

The Opening Door

will we say, 'No, you haven't really understood'? If so, we are going beyond the one who washed his disciples' feet and declared that the Kingdom of God was open to tax collectors and sinners.

What moves people so when they are at the limits of their humanity is, I believe, the experience of a certain kind of sadness. The sadness I am thinking about is not mournful, doleful, melancholic. It is not necessarily associated with the darker, more sorrowful side of life, although at its deepest level it has about it a hint of the tragic. It may be mixed with joy and glory and sheer wonder. Rather than be left downcast by such sadness, one is often elated by it, with a larger sense of the goodness of life, sometimes against all the odds. One's sense of belonging to the ongoing stream of life is affirmed by it.

When I first saw Rembrandt's *St Paul* in Washington's National Gallery my attention was drawn repeatedly to the apostle's left hand, resting on his knee. At that particular moment it seemed the most perfect thing I had ever seen. Later I was struck by Titian's ability to paint the human eye with a moisture, a luminosity, a clarity that is almost beyond belief. How is it that human beings are capable of such perfection, men and women who eat and sleep, who argue, love and make war, yet have it in them to produce a Rembrandt or a Titian who can move one so by the painting of a hand or an eye?

There is a kind of excellence, a type of beauty which moves us to tears, as when we listen to Jacqueline Du Pré playing the Elgar Cello Concerto, or sit quietly at the end of the play or book we have been reading and we know that something has gone out of us. That is the sadness I am talking about.

This sadness, this strange, wistful kind of sadness, that

The Presence of God

uplifts us with a sense of life's nobility, is implicit too in every close human relationship, parent and child, husband and wife, friend and friend. With the passage of time, the mountain-top experiences can have an exquisite pain about them in which we remember that we are not immortal and that sooner or later must come the parting. At first sight it would seem that this only points to tragedy, to broken hopes and to ultimate grief. Indeed it may. Yet it may also point in a totally different direction in which the real worth and glory of human relationships are seen in their true and ultimate light. Each human relationship, and the special sort of sadness involved in it, is an indicator of what really stands the test of time. It is rooted and grounded in love.

In his poem *An Arundel Tomb*, Philip Larkin describes the tomb of an earl and his lady in Chichester Cathedral. Side by side they lie, depicted in stone, the traditional small dogs at their feet; at first sight there seems nothing remarkable until the poet's eye catches

> . . . his left-hand gauntlet, still
> Clasped empty in the other; and
> One sees, with a sharp tender shock
> His hand, withdrawn, holding her hand.

Their stone faces are now disfigured and the passing centuries have changed entirely the world in which they once lived. But they who were once transient flesh and blood like ourselves remain linked together in stone. Amidst what I take to be precisely the sadness of which I have been writing, a disclosure occurs to the poet:

> Time has transfigured them into
> Untruth. The stone fidelity

The Opening Door

> They hardly meant has come to be
> Their final blazon, and to prove
> Our almost-instinct almost true:
> What will survive of us is love.[11]

Time and its passing, with its invitation to stand back from things in self-examination, is surely part of what it means to be human beings. It is hard to believe that anything else in this world has a similar ability, to rise above itself and to say with the aid of memory and anticipation, 'This is where I am; this is me.'

You may think that sadness is not quite the right word for what I am talking about. You may interpret it differently, give it another name. By whatever name we know it, it indicates that we are somehow touching the limits, we are beckoned away from ourselves towards something infinitely greater. And, although we have come by a strange route, we have arrived back at the Cotswold hills in autumn with which we began, for that too, was a limit situation in which I was confronted by unutterable beauty.

Simply to associate God with natural beauty alone distorts the picture, for in that Cotswold scene, stoats and foxes were also at work. Cruel things were happening alongside the apparently good. We too often take a 'soft' view of nature in religion: we have a tendency to romanticize, to try to tame something which may be downright hostile or, at best, only neutral to our interests. It is not self-evident from the world of nature that God is good. So do not misunderstand my reaction to that Cotswold day.

Nevertheless, like Mallory's mountain, 'because it's there', the natural world has the power to instil in us humility, stillness, wonder, fear, exhilaration and gratitude. We are at the

The Presence of God

limits of *our* humanity in the face of the natural world; it has the power to subdue us, even as, in other circumstances, we have the power to subdue it. That realization is the beginning of a movement of the human spirit upwards and outwards. It leads some to worship God and others to reach for their microscope.

When St Paul went to Athens he tried to point the Athenians to the God whom he believed lay behind their wisdom. 'God', he said, 'is not far from each one of us, for in him we live and move, in him we exist' (Acts 17.27). Within the limit situations common to our human experience there is the same God to whom the apostle witnessed. As we touch the edges of our humanity there is, I believe, the opening of doors and we touch and find God.

Conclusion

Relationships, story and ultimate situations with their special kind of sadness, are examples of what Peter Berger called 'signals of transcendence'.[12] They are common experiences which can point beyond themselves to a deeper reality.

Such experiences of God are not necessarily associated with obviously religious things. God will often take us by surprise. We will not always know how to react or quite where to place our response, particularly if we have always regarded ourselves as not in the least bit religious. Katherine Mansfield, in one of her letters in which she expressed her delight in a lovely spot in the Alps, wrote, 'If only one could make some small grasshoppery sound of praise to someone, thanks to someone – but who?'[13]

Connor Cruise O'Brien had no such reservations. He tells how his Roman Catholic mother prayed every day for ten

The Opening Door

years for his dead father in order to shorten his time in purgatory, or so she was told by the priests. It left O'Brien with a dislike of God that turned to disbelief. She had started praying on Christmas Day 1927 and ever after on Christmas Day O'Brien felt 'a kind of shiver', and always a horror of prayer.

In November 1978 his wife lay seriously ill in Jervis Street Hospital, Dublin after a car accident. The hospital was run by nuns and was full of kindness and prayer. It was on Christmas Day that he knew his wife would get better.

> She was going to be alright. Thank God. It didn't matter a damn whether I believed in God or not, or even whether I wanted to thank Him. I was just thanking Him anyway; and I noticed something.
>
> The old shiver, inseparable from every Christmas Day over exactly half a century, had clean gone. I had often read 'The Ancient Mariner', but that Christmas morning in St Agnes Ward, I *was* that venerable seafarer. That damned bird had gone! There was nothing round my neck any more!
>
> The self-same moment I could pray.[14]

4 Our Response to God

Important though an experience of God is, it is never enough in itself. It requires the complement of response. Sought after for its own sake it is merely self-indulgence. Interpreted aright, it becomes a signal indeed, a beckoning, a calling.

As I have tried to answer the question, 'Where are the opening doors which lead to God?' I have been driven to see that most often they lie in commonplace experiences because God himself is not remote, austere, majestic, but is rather the opposite, enmeshed as he is in what is close at hand; he is homely, ordinary, poor and often nameless. The abiding sign of the nature of God is Jesus who had his origins in Nazareth, which to Nathanael was a real stumbling-block. But Jesus in his ordinariness called forth the very best in people. At least his everyday kind of divinity challenged people's motives, goals, values and actions at a level which they could understand and he gave them the opportunity to do something about it, not in some far-away future but there and then in their ordinary lives. At the same time he opened up men and women to a larger world, the world of God's resources which were available to them, resources which issued in love, forgiveness and sacrificial service.

The Opening Door

I take Jesus as the touchstone by which to interpret our experiences of God. Not that we always get things right. Recognition is at the heart of the matter and, as the first disciples demonstrated after the resurrection, we will not always recognize that God is with us.

Nevertheless, the ordinariness of Jesus challenges us at the level of our ordinariness. So, finally we turn to our response which can only be rooted in our everyday experiences. What is the manner of our being Christian in response to the God who hides himself? How do we understand our prayers, our practical response, in the light of the God of the commonplace? And what does it mean to have faith in such a God?

(a) Prodigal sons and daughters

The story of the apparently selfish younger son who wastes his money in the far country and goes home with his tail between his legs is one of the most popular in the Gospels (Luke 15.11–32). We normally adopt a disapproving air at the boy's selfishness and his irresponsibility once he has got his hands on his share of the farm. When he returns home a beaten man we shake our heads wisely as if to say, 'That's how it always is. People always know where they are best off. Look how generous the father was to his young tearaway son!'

Strange things happen, however, when you lift the story out of its religious setting and give it to a group of sixth-formers for example, as a case-study in family relationships. Surely the younger son was right to try to stand on his own feet? That is what most teenagers have to learn to do and what most parents will encourage. His misfortune was that he did not have sufficient maturity to cope with the difficulties. He caved in when he ought to have stuck it out. Worst of all, the experience of the famine drove him home not as a *son* but as a *slave*. He admits as much himself: 'I am no longer worthy to be called your son; treat me as one of your hired servants.' He had not grown up after all, and, although it was natural for him to come home, he did so for the wrong reason. He was coming back to the security of the fold, into the same dull, immature, servant role from which his elder brother had not had the imagination even to try to escape.

Only the father could save him from himself. 'No, my boy,' we seem to hear the father say, 'I don't want you as my slave, I've plenty of those. I want you as my son. As a sign of that, here is my ring and the finest robe in the house!' The feast of the fatted calf then becomes not just a celebration of the prodigal's return, it is the mark of the father's hope that the boy will become a man.

The most significant task of parents is to enable their children to find sufficient maturity to stand as persons in their own right, distinct from the parents who have given them life. In that process of growing up, which inevitably means growing apart, the potential for conflict is endless. Children will be angry with their parents, seeing their limitations and their faults. They will argue increasingly about what their parents tell them to do and resist the doing of it. For their part, parents will learn new ways, perhaps truer ways, of retaining the love and affection of their children, love which is freely given rather than demanded or simply offered in a childish need for security.

In this growing up there is always a large measure of growing away. Children gradually distance themselves from their parents, a process often expressed by leaving home, just like the prodigal. The ultimate aim is that parents and children

The Opening Door

come to see each other as persons in their own right, autonomous within a voluntary interdependence.

If we insist on calling God our father, as Jesus teaches us we should, we ought not to shrink from the implications of the family life we already know. An over-demanding authoritarian parent will break a child's spirit and render him or her less than a full person, or else that person will rebel utterly and hate the parent. Either way their relationship will be filled with anxiety and guilt.

Similarly, a stern, authoritarian, high-profile, punitive god will enslave people or drive them to disbelief. This is the god of so much popular religious imagination and it is the Aunt Sally of the secular critic too. He has no substance really. He is an idol, an image of man in god, a projection of our own power-seeking, Freud's exalted father. He has no substance, but he has been given enormous power by the prodigals who return home as his slaves. They have forfeited their full maturity, handing over responsibility for themselves and as a result live with guilt, fear and superstition.

Enslavement to such a god will often mean a retreat to medievalism. When the south transept of York Minster was badly damaged by fire on 8th July 1984, two days after the consecration of the controversial Bishop of Durham, there were those who said that it was God's judgment on a church that was becoming doctrinally soft. Medievalism like this not only allows for a punitive god who deals out thunderbolts to the unwise, the unrighteous or the unsound, it encourages belief in a world inhabited by evil spirits and in the need for exorcism. As such, it nicely coincides with all those elements of folk-religion and superstition which lie just beneath the surface of the subconscious and which once let loose, will lay waste so many human lives.

Our Response to God

It is a far cry from the New Testament picture of Jesus, which, when you have allowed for the fact that the telling of the story is two thousand years old, reveals a Father God who is prepared to be rejected and crucified and who does not retaliate. He is the wise parent whose love for the children is undying, but he will not foist his love upon them. If they will have it at all, they must do so willingly. So God's continuing presence with men and women is quiet and humble, mostly unseen, always discreet and waiting to be recognized. The relationship which he seeks is not that of the master and slave but of the parent with his or her children where the bond between them is not fear but love.

It is in this sense that we are all potentially prodigal sons and daughters. In the process of our growing up we may cave in, fearful in a hostile world, seeking the easy securities of a comfortable but ultimately enslaving god. Or in our growing apart we may come home to a true appreciation of our heavenly Father, whose characteristic mark is humility, in whose service there is perfect freedom, and love of whom banishes fear.

Of this difference between bondage and freedom, slavery and sonship, St Paul has written the following and his words appear to be an appropriate comment on the parable of the Prodigal Son: 'The Spirit you have received is not a spirit of slavery leading you back into a life of fear, but a Spirit that makes us sons, enabling us to cry "Abba! Father!"' (Rom. 8.15). The transition from fear to love, from slavery to sonship, involves death at a profound level. T. S. Eliot's wise man returned from Christ's nativity in a strange country unsure of the difference between birth and death:

The Opening Door

> . . . this Birth was
> Hard and bitter agony for us, like Death, our death.
> We returned to our places, these Kingdoms,
> But no longer at ease here, in the old dispensation,
> With an alien people clutching their gods.
> I should be glad of another death.[1]

For Christians, that transition which is called resurrection is made in the company of Jesus who is our brother and who, in his very ordinariness, is the symbol of God. It is he who reveals the essential friendliness of the universe and who assures us that it is our birthright to be sons and daughters of God.

There is an unexpected consequence of this discovery that we are all potential prodigals who return home not as slaves but as sons and daughters. We are freed from competitiveness. The rivalry that existed in the Prodigal's home was natural enough. But it might have been less embittered if the elder son could have had the grace to accept the father's assurance that the younger boy was indeed his brother and that whatever happened his, the elder brother's, place in the home was safe.

Competitiveness dogs the church at every hand. My doctrine is purer than yours; my denomination has more of the light than your denomination; my Christianity is nearer the truth than your Islam. Like the elder son, we are jealous of our rights and privileges, over-protective of our position, and unwilling to grant recognition to other returning prodigals. As in all families, such a reaction mostly stems from insecurity, from an as yet immature understanding of our place within the home.

Some of the great masters of the religious experience teach

Our Response to God

us to have more confidence. In his *Asian Journal* the Trappist monk, Thomas Merton, tells of his visit to the giant Buddhas of Polonnaruwa in Ceylon. His description seems the ultimate experience of the God of many names and of none:

> ... the silence of the extraordinary faces. The great smiles. Huge and yet subtle. Filled with every possibility, questioning nothing, knowing everything, rejecting nothing, the peace not of emotional refutation . . . that has seen through every question without trying to discredit anyone or anything . . . Surely, with Mahabalipuram and Polonnaruwa my Asian pilgrimage has come clear and purified itself. I mean, I know and have seen what I was obscurely looking for. I don't know what else remains but I have now seen and have pierced through the surface and have got beyond the shadow and the disguise.[2]

Within days, Thomas Merton was dead.

(b) Commonplace spirituality

After questions about God and suffering and the problems arising out of personal relationships, the question which seems to recur most frequently is 'How do I pray?' People do not have time, have never learned, do not feel it works, cannot understand it, or consider it to be unnecessary or inappropriate. But everywhere there are hints of an apparent contradiction. Many people have problems with prayers but continue praying. Twenty years ago, Michel Quoist's *Prayers of Life*[3] became popular because they offered a way through the contradiction. They neither looked nor felt like prayers but one was assuredly praying them. Michel Quoist himself described them in his preface as 'meditations on life'. Beginning with a telephone, a swing, or a five-pound note, he gradually widens the circle of his thought to include God, himself and others. His method of praying is summed up in his own words: 'The Father has put us into the world, not to walk through it with lowered eyes, but to search for him through things, events, people. Everything must reveal God to us.'[4] Such an approach to praying is not to be regarded as second-best, an easier path for those who find the discipline of 'real prayer' too hard. It is a recognition of the God who is hidden in commonplace things, who can be known in everyday experiences, because that is his nature. He is only being true to himself.

Don Shockley, Chaplain at Emory University, Atlanta, has recently developed this theme in an article entitled 'The Shopping Mall Mystic'. Although he had rejected early on the traditional prayer life taught him as a child, he now realizes that he has nevertheless practised 'an unconscious spiritual discipline'. As a young student pastor in rural Alabama, he left his sermon preparation to the last moment because of the pressure of academic life, and would often complete the sermon on Sunday morning in the local 'donut' shop. This habit of writing his sermons in cafés, truck stops and other public places continued, no matter how well prepared beforehand he was, because he discovered that something often happened which would contribute directly to the theme.

Things came to a head during the season of Advent, when the waitress in the coffee shop noted his scribbling with increasing apprehension and came over to accuse him of being an undercover agent of the company sent to evaluate how she was doing her job. When he assured her that he was

Our Response to God

not, she turned to leave with the words, 'I'm sure glad you are not one of those *expecters!*'

I went away from the scene in a mood of exhilaration, thinking of myself in a new way; in my imagination I had acquired the position of Chief Expecter, with primary responsibility for entering all sorts of public establishments for the purpose of listening and looking at the ordinary, everyday human scene with the expectation that a mysterious dimension of depth would reveal itself in direct proportion to my readiness to receive it.

Following that episode I began to practise a kind of meditation in all sorts of places where human traffic is flowing: in addition to restaurants of all kinds, I have done much of this in trains, planes, shopping malls, waiting-rooms, museums, parks and other such places. Listening and looking, letting my mind run free, I write whatever comes. I have often been surprised by the thoughts and words which appear on the paper before me. Gradually, I have come to recognize this somewhat odd behaviour as the form which prayer has taken in my life. Sometimes these free-flowing expressions, ranging from almost ecstatic outbursts of joy to agonizing questions at the brink of bitterness, are addressed directly to God. More often they are not. Nevertheless, for me the experience has come to be a kind of spirituality which seems to transform the mundane, commercial spheres into Sacred spaces or, perhaps, to open up the essential holiness of the commonplace.[5]

Commonplace spirituality led Don Shockley on to one further, perhaps more basic, discovery. He needed times of disengagement and quietness, even if some of those times were in busy places! He may have rejected the kind of spirituality which had nurtured him as a youth but, by a totally different route, he had rediscovered its essential purpose.

Prayer is the sign of a relationship; it indicates a frame of mind. Prayer, and our search for it through times of quietness, particularly when we are busy and under stress, is our acknowledgment that we have understood, however dimly, that life is not bounded by our own humanity. There are other dimensions which include our fellow men and women and that mystery we call God. Through prayer we tap resources of energy, resilience, compassion and illumination, not just for ourselves but for others, as we become aware of the strange sensitivities that prayer creates.

Commonplace spirituality affirms this no less than other kinds of prayer. It resists an unearthed piety but embraces a down-to-earth God. It does not replace traditional praying but neither is it an easy second-best. It is also the necessary complement of another aspect of Christian life, one which has all the appearance of real spirituality for increasing numbers of people, that of service or involvement.

Sadly, prayer and action are frequently set in opposition to one another. Prayer is all too often seen as inward-looking, an almost selfish act of withdrawal from the world of people and affairs. For those who view prayer like this, action becomes the only worthwhile response, the complete opposite of what they see as useless self-centred prayer. Better to get things done in God's name, to put Christ's teaching into practice, rather than to worry unduly about the health of our spiritual lives.

This is a very damaging view of the relationship of prayer and action, but it is not the only way of looking at things by any means. Rather than setting prayer and action in conflict or seeing them as separate and different responses to God, the

Our Response to God

one 'spiritual' and the other 'practical', I prefer to see them as two aspects of the same response which we move in and out of our whole life through. Sometimes prayer will mean more to us than action; sometimes it will be the other way round and then we will discover that true service is not to be dismissed as mere 'Activism'. Christian service, work for Christ's sake, labour, committed action has all the validity of prayer simply because it is a response to the hidden, down-to-earth God. We cannot ignore the fact that for many of our contemporaries the needs of the hungry, the poor, the homeless, the broken, are opening doors which lead to a greater discovery of the God who has embraced our common humanity in all its weakness. Their spiritual life and their whole understanding of God will almost certainly be nurtured by prayer either of the traditional kind or that of the Shopping Mall Mystic. But equally it cannot fail to include the committed response of action in which, whether through success or failure, they encounter the living God.

Several years ago, the church which I am presently serving established a link with another Methodist church in London's East End. At first we in Oxford probably felt that as rather privileged, well-placed Christians we had a lot to offer our brothers and sisters in Poplar. We set to work to raise money to support one of our own student members who worked there for a year; we collected second-hand clothes for sale in the church's bazaars; the students of our church organized holiday play-schemes for the children of the area. It began to feel as if we were doing what we could to support our fellow Christians in a more difficult area, although in all conscience, what we were doing was little enough. But we were doing it and that had to be a good thing. What we were not expecting was the effect it would have on us. One or two students who

The Opening Door

had taken an active part in the 'Poplar Link' began seriously to think about their future careers as they watched committed men and women, both lay and ordained, at work in an area which seemed hard-going but tremendously rewarding in its own way. Would their careers take them into areas where their qualifications would find most success in terms of money and prospects or were there real alternatives where people counted just as much? What began as straightforward service, awakened by obvious need, deepened into a real spirituality and an experience of God.

Neither was the church as a whole left untouched. Becoming what we all thought of as a Good Samaritan, albeit rather at arm's length, led us to appreciate that Christian presence in an area does not depend upon large numbers, upon obvious success or upon guaranteed income. But it does need a willingness to be there, whatever the cost, to listen to what people in stressful conditions have to say, because in listening to them one might just catch echoes of another voice saying, 'When I was hungry, when I was thirsty ... where were you?' The result was that the whole church community began to ask questions about its life and witness at the city centre, questions to which we are slowly finding answers. The point is this: that what at one time seemed to be a piece of 'mere' action deepened into service which in time threatened to become real spirituality, real response to God.

The South American theologian, Gustavo Gutierrez, writing on the much more important scale of Christians standing alongside the world's poor in their struggle against poverty and impersonality has written this:

Living and thinking the faith from within the immurement of the 'wretched of the earth' will lead us along paths where

Our Response to God

we shall not meet the great ones of this world. Instead we shall meet the Lord, we shall meet him in the poor of Latin America and of other continents. And like the disciples at Emmaus, we shall interpret his words and his deeds in the light of Easter, and our eyes will be opened.[6]

Against that perspective, the acts of kindness and service that you and I are capable of seem small indeed. The massive heroism of Archbishop Oscar Romero, who was assassinated in San Salvador in April 1980 for standing alongside the poor of his country in Christian service, is way beyond anything that most of us are called upon to give. And yet it may well be that the widow's mite of our own service, or the tireless patience of the social worker, teacher or nurse, draw their inspiration from the same source and are a recognition of the God who 'pitches his tent' in the midst of common humanity (see John 1.14).

It is at this point that prayer and action are not two conflicting or even contrasting responses to the experience of God but are modes of the same response. Indeed, prayer passes into action and action is transmuted into prayer in a single realization that if we can know him at all it will be in the commonplace realities of suffering, joy, hope, despair and ... people.

(c) Faith

The characteristic way in which we relate to the God we experience is by faith. And yet there is no word surrounded by more mystique than 'faith'. It is a hard word to understand, involving belief in impossible things, a suspension of our normal thought processes. It is a code-word, a password

The Opening Door

almost, that admits us to some strange inner circle where things are done differently. The very word which most truly expresses what we believe about God has become a barrier to many. The more we try to make 'faith' a special word, a holy word, one which separates those who have it from those who do not, the more we declare that we have totally missed the point of the Word become flesh. The God who hides himself in common things, who is quietly disclosed through the opening doors which I have attempted to describe, is most truly known through faith. But this faith does not ask the impossible. It too is rooted in the common things of life.

First of all, let me attempt to draw a distinction between faith and belief. If we were asked to describe our belief, our reply might well take the form of the old creeds of the church: 'I believe in God the Father, in Jesus Christ, in the Holy Spirit . . .'

Faith is not irrational or incoherent. It has content. There is something to believe in and although it is impossible to prove, it nevertheless can be thought through intelligently. Faith includes our belief but goes beyond it, for rather more than our intellect is called for. When the psalmist first looked up into the night sky and marvelled (Psalm 8), there was a movement of the whole person upwards and away from himself as the centre of things, towards a reality that confronted him in the immensity of space.

When C. S. Lewis set out one morning to go to Whipsnade Zoo, he did not believe that Jesus was the Son of God. When he arrived, he did. What had taken place during the journey was not an intellectual change – that had been going on for a long time. It was something that belonged to the whole of him, not just the rational part, not just the emotional part, nor yet that portion of him that responded to the mysterious

Our Response to God

presence of God. What happened involved the whole of him offered to God in what can only be called faith.

Faith, then, is quite different from the content of our belief. It is deeper, more personal, taking its inspiration, its character, from the hundred-and-one different experiences of life which come to us. Faith is the mainspring of our lives; faith is that which lifts us up when we are down once again; faith is that which sustains us and renews us when world-weariness and cynicism wash over us like an ebb-tide; faith is that which reaches down into us and calls forth the best when it would be easier to offer the tawdry and the second rate.

Faith is deeply personal, it is part of our very being which we find hard to describe but which we know is there.

There are several ways in which I would like to approach this key element in our lives. They are not religious in the normal sense of that word and yet, in their different ways, each points to an important, underlying sense of the presence of God.

Starting again is a very common human experience. It can be an invigorating experience after a holiday, or in the New Year, or at a new job. There is release from the past, more space to look afresh and perhaps to try a new approach. Starting again can be a chastening experience, painful even. Relationships falter, become difficult to maintain, require a complete break or a new start.

Whatever the cost, individuals do start again, put painful experiences behind them, overcome handicaps and learn to cope with that part of themselves which is broken or scarred. That jockey who was nursed back to health after life-threatening cancer; that motor-racing star who broke every bone in his body but who somehow recovered to race again; that tennis-player who cannot control his temper or

The Opening Door

his tongue, who has to face his family or his public afterwards; that man or woman who one day takes stock and says: 'It's not good enough; I need to start again.'

Men and women can start again, whatever the circumstances, or as Jesus put it, they can be born anew (John 3.3), although I would not want to reserve that phrase for a meaning which is narrowly religious.

The more I think about starting again, the more I realize that it requires a certain space between us and events and into that space is poured the grace of God, although often we will not recognize it at the time. Starting again in a job, a relationship, an outlook on life or even a personality needs that breathing-space between us and events so that we begin to realize that life is not always inevitable, sometimes we can change direction. That is an experience of faith; it goes right to the heart of our whole being and the God who inspires it, simply because he is hidden in life itself, need not be named.

Alternatively, we may think of faith as experienced and nurtured in our reaction to life's surprises. Some of life's best moments are those which take us completely by surprise. They are quite literally godsends. We have to work for many things. Often there is no alternative and after the planning and the effort, the results begin to flow and we experience the satisfaction of achievement. But equally, there are moments which spring out upon us, moments which we could not have foreseen, which cannot be worked for or bought. Those are the moments which have to be experienced there and then because they cannot be prolonged, recorded or videoed, only treasured and the memory of them stored in the heart. They are pure serendipity.

Surprise is part and parcel of the gospel story; Mary surprised at the message of the angel, the shepherds surprised to

Our Response to God

find him lying in a stable, Nathanael surprised that anything good could come from Nazareth, Zacchaeus surprised that Jesus singled him out in the crowd, the centurion surprised at the manner of Jesus' dying, the women surprised that the stone was rolled away.

In the Christian year, the time of harvest is a reminder of the godsends. They have probably been staring us in the face all the time and suddenly we realize they are there. The love of a friend is like that. It is there all the time, constant, often low-key, always looking for our good, putting in a good word behind our back, smoothing the way unbeknown to us, and then suddenly it bursts upon us. 'Is that really for me!' we exclaim. 'Have you honestly done that for me – I don't deserve it.'

So, too, we may live oblivious of God's presence or careless of him. We may be struggling to make sense of the bad things that have suddenly come upon us, we may be so busy at a crucial point in our lives or we may have reached some kind of plateau where life does not seem so hard. Then suddenly we will come upon him and we 'know that all will be well, and all manner of things shall be well'.

Thirdly, I would like to suggest that faith, in the words of one New Testament writer, 'gives substance to our hopes, and makes us certain of realities we do not see' (Heb. 11.1). Although it may not seem so, that experience of faith is also rooted and grounded in things close at hand. I once stood in a church building that was being renovated. As a sanctuary it was unrecognizable for it was no more than a building-site with four walls and a roof. The floor was up, the balcony removed, the pulpit and Communion table were no more. Water was washing the external walls and, worryingly, some of the internal ones as well. An excavator was attacking the

The Opening Door

last few pieces of resisting concrete. I could not possibly see how this building-site could be turned into a usable church again. But in the old minister's vestry were a set of plans that assured me it could be done. Those plans were the architect's vision of how things would turn out, they gave 'substance to our hopes' and made us certain of unseen realities!

It is said that it was while he was in France during the last war, with destruction all around him and those lovely French churches standing out on the skyline, that Basil Spence decided that if he survived the war he would build a cathedral. The result was Coventry Cathedral. Around him was all the mayhem but Basil Spence held on to the future and turned the jagged, pointless, fragments of life into a whole.

That visionary skill is possessed by architects to a special degree but it is not peculiar to them. All of us are capable of visions of what might be, ideas of how things should be. The difficulty is holding on to them, making the visions and the ideas work when we feel the inner resources being slowly sapped from us by cynicism and hard reality. For many people, faith is making something worthwhile out of the circumstances of their lives, when those circumstances are far from ideal. It is holding on to the vision of what things might become.

It was faith of this kind that was displayed by the old lady who told me how she got married during the First World War. Her fiancé was a military doctor, back from the Front on two weeks' sick-leave in 1917 and she a nurse in a military hospital in this country. In the middle of the war to end wars with apparently no hope for the future to speak of, the two of them married. It was an act of sheer faith in love and in life. It does not need to be claimed for God in so many words. We should not be so uncertain of ourselves or of God that no faith

Our Response to God

is allowed unless it carries a specifically religious tag. The God who is hidden in humanity will so often remain unnamed, unremarked, but it is he who inspires such faith none the less.

If it be objected that life does not often merit such faith, that more often it deals falsely with us or that one can only talk optimistically about faith and love from the sheltered comfort of one's armchair, then I turn once more to Gustavo Gutierrez, whose thinking about God is done in the squalor and terror of some of the poorest countries of South America. He writes:

> Faith is confidence in love. It is faith in the Father who loved us first, without any merit of our own, and who fills our life with love and largeness.[7]

Taken all in all, faith in God is an attitude to things. It is a stance that we take over against life itself and we act accordingly. There is no magic to it, no mystique. Faith requires no mental gymnastics; it is not separated from the rest of our experience by a fence of holy barbed wire. Faith is understood and practised in the humanities of life, in its tragedies and triumphs both small and great.

Suppose, finally, I could discover someone, in fact or in fiction, who could bring all the different strands of faith together in himself. Suppose I could find someone who could help me start all over again, who could speak to my innermost self, who was so sensitive that he could reveal the deepest reality in ordinary things, who taught a rugged common sense and yet could inspire in me the noblest ideals. Suppose I could encounter someone who could embody all these things and much more besides – what would he have to be like?

The Opening Door

Would he be much different from the man before whom Thomas knelt in faith.

That is what it means for me to have faith and to call Jesus the Son of God.

Conclusion

In these four short chapters I have tried to understand how we experience God. The central conviction is that God is hidden in everyday life, implicit in all our experiences and in all the relationships between people. He rarely seems obvious, apparently preferring ministry to strength, weakness to power, silence to self-publicity. Recognition is at the heart of things and patience the prerequisite of recognition. If we experience God at all, it is not our doing, it is a gift, a surprise.

Many things are said and done in the name of God, some of them with terrible effect in the lives of men and women. We often claim too much for him, make him responsible for things which are plainly not his responsibility, elevate ourselves or our own concerns and call them 'god'. For these reasons we need great humility when we talk of him. As Martin Buber wrote: 'We cannot cleanse the word "God" and we cannot make it whole; but defiled and mutilated as it is, we can raise it from the ground and set over it an hour of great care.'[8]

There is a story told about Moses in the Book of Exodus in which he wanted to see God face to face (Ex. 33.18–23). He had after all brought the Children of Israel out of Egypt and through the wilderness at God's command, a difficult and demanding job. He obviously felt that he had a right to ask. It is said that God did indeed pass before Moses, but not before he had hidden Moses in a cleft of the rock and covered

Our Response to God

him with his hand. 'You shall see my back', declared God, 'but my face shall not be seen.'

It is for that reason that all our talk about God will be in stories and symbols and at best will only be a tentative alternative to silence. And it is for that reason also that all our experiences of him will be fleeting, laden with ambiguity and will come to us as quietly and as unobtrusively as a door silently swinging open.

St Augustine was aware of the difficulties of talking to others about God. But he also recalled the promise of his presence when he wrote:

> What man will give another man the understanding of this, or what angel will give another angel, or what angel will give a man? Of You we must ask, in You we must seek, at You we must knock. Thus only shall we receive, thus shall we find, thus will it be opened to us.[9]

We may not recognize him. Often we shall be so taken up with our own concerns that we shall miss the presence of God completely. But if we live with hands open to receive he will be able to give. It may be that we shall touch only the hem of his garment but it will be enough to convince us that the reality behind all realities is God.

Notes

Page 33   Harold Kushner
Page 50 - God's presence.
Page 86.

Notes

Preface

1. Martin Buber, *Biblical Humanism*, MacDonald 1968, p. 3.

Chapter 1 The Silence of God

1. Percy Young, *Elgar, O.M.*, Collins 1955. The italics are mine.
2. Shelley, 'Adonais', *Poetical Works*, ed. Thomas Hutchinson, Oxford University Press 1970, LII p. 443.
3. Canon Charles Elliott, BBC Radio, 27 January 1983.
4. Robert Davidson, *The Courage to Doubt*, SCM Press 1983.
5. Michael Goulder & John Hick, *Why Believe in God?*, SCM Press 1983, p. 28.
6. Matthew Arnold, *The Poetical Works of Matthew Arnold*, ed. C. B. Tinker & H. F. Lowry, Oxford University Press 1950, p. 246.
7. Bel Mooney, 'Scapegoat in a Country Churchyard', *The Sunday Times*, 27 December 1981.
8. Simone Weil, *Waiting on God*, Collins 1978, p. 17.
9. Ibid., p. 42.
10. *The Times*, 26 April 1984. © Times Newspapers Ltd.
11. Frederick Houk Borsch, *Power in Weakness*, Fortress Press 1983, p. 107. Lines from T. S. Eliot, *East Coker*, are reprinted by permission of Faber & Faber Ltd and Harcourt Brace Jovanovich Inc.
12. Wallace Stevens, *Collected Poems*, Vintage Books 1982, p. 386. Reprinted by permission of Faber & Faber Ltd and Alfred A. Knopf Inc.

Notes

Chapter 2 The Ambiguity of God

1. Thomas Merton, *The Wisdom of the Desert*, Sheldon Press 1961, p. 54.
2. A. N. Whitehead, *Process and Reality*, Cambridge University Press 1929, pp. 484-5.
3. Frederick Houk Borsch, *Power in Weakness*, p. 121.
4. Harold S. Kushner, *When Bad Things Happen to Good People*, Avon Books, New York 1981. Copyright © 1981 by Harold S. Kushner. Reprinted by permission of Schocken Books Inc.
5. Ibid., p. 140.
6. Ibid., p. 148.
7. Dorothee Soelle, *Suffering*, Fortress Press 1975.
8. Kushner, ibid., p. 85.
9. Henri Nouwen, *Clowning in Rome*, Image Books 1979. Copyright © 1979 by Henri Nouwen. Reprinted by permission of Doubleday & Co. Inc.
10. Ibid., p. 2.
11. Elizabeth Jennings, 'The Clown', *Song for a Birth and a Death*, Andre Deutsch 1961, p. 38. Reprinted by permission of David Higham Associates Ltd.
12. Malcolm Muggeridge, *Something Beautiful for God*, Fontana 1971, p. 74.

Chapter 3 The Presence of God

1. R. S. Thomas, *Laboratories of the Spirit*, Macmillan 1975, p. 60. Reprinted by permission.
2. A. N. Whitehead, *Religion in the Making!*, Cambridge University Press 1926, p. 16.
3. 'Death without Concealment', *British Medical Journal* No. 6307, December 1981, p. 1629.
4. John V. Taylor, *The Go-between God*, SCM Press 1972, p. 126.
5. John Wren Lewis, 'Modern Philosophy and the Doctrine of the Trinity', *Philosophical Quarterly*, June 1955, p. 223.
6. Ian Ramsey, *Christian Empiricism*, Sheldon Press 1974, p. 159.
7. T. W. Manson, *The Teaching of Jesus*, Cambridge University Press 1955, p. 73.
8. Sally McFague, *Speaking in Parables*, Fortress Press 1975, pp. 76-7.
9. Evelyn Waugh, *Brideshead Revisited*, Penguin 1981, p. 395. Reprinted by permission of A. D. Peters & Co. Ltd.

Notes

10. Jürgen Moltmann, *The Experience of God*, SCM Press 1980, pp. 8–9.
11. Philip Larkin, 'An Arundel Tomb', *The Whitsun Weddings*, Faber & Faber 1983, p. 45. Reprinted by permission.
12. Peter L. Berger, *A Rumour of Angels*, Pelican Books 1971, p. 70. Copyright © Peter L. Berger 1969. Reprinted by permission of Penguin Books.
13. Quoted by John Baillie, *Our Knowledge of God*, Oxford University Press 1958, p. 249. Used by permission of The Society of Authors.
14. Conor Cruise O'Brien, *The Observer*, 4 June 1979.

Chapter 4 Our Response to God

1. T. S. Eliot, 'Journey of the Magi', *Collected Poems 1909–1935*, Faber & Faber 1959, p. 108. Reprinted by permission of Faber & Faber Ltd.
2. *The Asian Journal of Thomas Merton*, ed. Naomi Burton, Brother Patrick Hart & James Laughlin, Sheldon Press 1974, pp. 233–6.
3. Michel Quoist, *Prayers of Life*, Gill and Macmillan 1963. Reprinted by permission.
4. Ibid., p. 14.
5. Don Shockley, 'Shopping Mall Mystic', *The Light Shines in Darkness*, Scriptures for the Church Seasons Series, Graded Press 1976, pp. 27–8. Copyright © 1976 by Graded Press. Used by permission.
6. Gustavo Guttierez, *The Power of the Poor in History*, SCM Press 1983, p. 214.
7. Ibid., p. 20.
8. Martin Buber, *The Eclipse of God*, Harvester Press 1979, p. 8.
9. *Confessions of St. Augustine*, trans. F. J. Sheed, Sheed & Ward 1944, p. 290.